Pieces of the Past

by Nancy J. Martin

featuring quilt designs by Marsha McCloskey

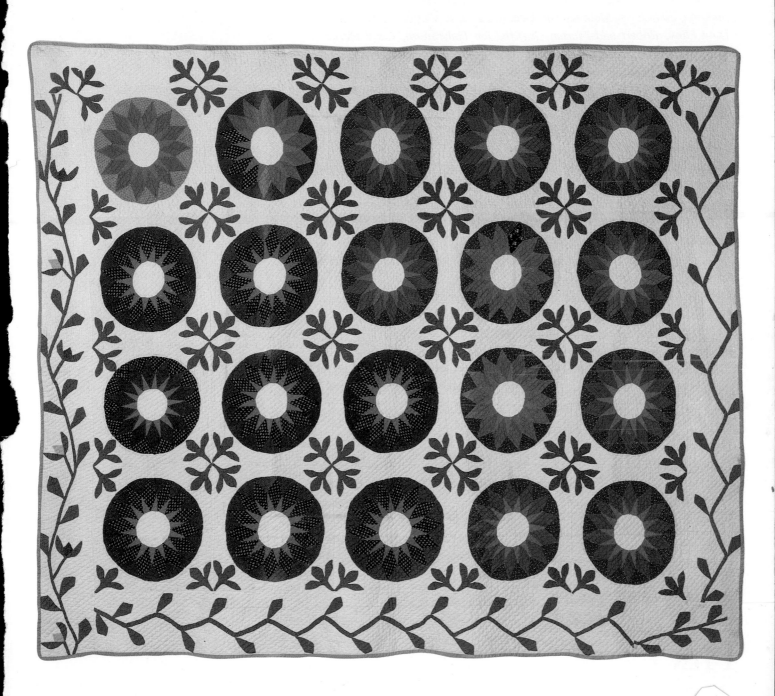

That Patchwork Place, Inc., Bothell, Washington
Second Edition, 1986

Frontispiece: **Setting Sun** by Ellen Bestow Vinning:, c. 1833, Connecticut, 76 1/2" x 89". This intricately pieced scrap quilt journeyed westward with its maker to Illinois, then was given to heirs in Washington. (Collection of Rosalie Pfeifer, Kent, Washington)

ACKNOWLEDGEMENTS

Special thanks are extended to the many quiltmakers and collectors who graciously loaned their quilts to be photographed:

Lillian Burch, Dottie Charlson, Diane Coombs, Dick and Nancy Dice, Pat Dunning, Judy Eide, Maurene and George Edwards, Donna Hanson Eines, Tony Flink, Robert and Marian Griffith, Jan Halgrimson, Carol Harker, Suzanne Hammond, Sara and Steven Martin, Marsha McCloskey, Edward and Sylvia McFadden, Marjorie L. Meyers, Jack and Sylvia Mittendorf, Lois Odell, Carolann Palmer, Eldra Pebsworth, Joyce Penington, Rosalie Pfiefer, Pam Reising (Comforts of Home), Sue Saltkill, Joanne Starr, Stearns and Foster Company, Peg Storey, Shirley Thompson, Nancyann Johanson Twelker, and Carol Walkky;

The Museum of History and Industry, Seattle, Washington and photographer Howard R. Giske and curatorial assistant Lois Bark for their help in photographing selected quilts from the museum's collection;

Bonnie Leman, QUILTER'S NEWSLETTER MAGAZINE, for the photo of the Colonial History Quilt;

Carolann Palmer, for generously loaning her collection of vintage quilting patterns, scrapbooks and catalogs.

Freda Smith, Andrea Scadden, and Judy Eide for their fine quilting and Georgina Fries whose quilting service proved invaluable.

Although most of the quilts in PIECES OF THE PAST have not been published before, a few have appeared in other That Patchwork Place publications, and five photographs were supplied by Cyril Nelson from THE QUILT ENGAGEMENT CALENDAR TREASURY and THE 1985 QUILT ENGAGEMENT CALENDAR, published by E.P. Dutton.

Credits:

Photography . . . . *Carl Murray*
Howard Giske, Museum of History and Industry
Illustration and Graphics . . . . *Stephanie Benson*
Photographic Settings . . . . *Judy Thomas*
Jan Whalen, Wicker Works
Sherry Johnson, Country Goose

That Patchwork Place ™

PIECES OF THE PAST ©

©Nancy J. Martin, 1986

CONTENTS

Snowball, made by Nancy Martin, 1985, Woodinville, Washington, 40" x 58". Quilted by Andrea Scadden. (Collection of That Patchwork Place, Inc., Bothell, Washington)

PREFACE

As I view old quilts, I always wonder about the maker and why she chose those particular fabrics and that special pattern. Why did she use a differing fabric for only one block? Was the mistake on another block deliberate or intentional? Were those scraps of fabric from her family's clothing? How long did it take her to quilt this masterpiece? Where did she find the time? Was this quilt ever used by her family? So many questions unanswered.... If only quilts could talk, what marvelous information they could give us, what wonderful stories they might be able to tell.

In searching for answers to the many questions I had about old quilts, I decided to record my findings in a book, *Pieces of the Past.*

Researching the history of a particular quilt is a long and arduous task since documentation of quilts has been very sparse. Nonetheless, quilt historians and study groups have gathered information on textiles, fabrics, and quilt patterns that help us determine the period in which a quilt may have been made. I am indebted to them for their research.

Interviews with long-time quilters, diaries, magazines, and excerpts from earlier novels give us an insight into the lives of the women who made these quilts. However, the average woman's domestic life and needlework projects were never considered an adequate subject for more specialized research or historical records. Susan Strasser's history of American housework *Never Done*, is the exception and has proved invaluable. *Pieces of the Past* is not an historical work; it is an attempt to relate history to the lives of early quilters. With difficulty, I resisted the temptation to make generalizations which serve theory and perpetuate the quilting myths and legends that have so long existed.

Has this exercise of historical imagination provided truth? If only quilts could talk, what marvelous information they could give us, what wonderful stories they might be able to tell.

Nancy Martin

Diversion, made by Nancy Martin, 1985, Woodinville, Washington, 55 1/2" x 55 1/2". Quilted by Freda Smith. (Collection of That Patchwork Place, Inc., Bothell, Washington)

4

INTRODUCTION

This book has three parts. The first section explores the history of quilt patterns, colors, and fabrics in the United States. Both antique and contemporary quilts made in the traditional style are used throughout the text.

The second section of the book, written by Marsha McCloskey, tells how to make contemporary quilts in a traditional style, along with helpful information on quilt design and fabric selection.

The third part of *Pieces of the Past* is the pattern section. Quilt blocks are grouped according to size or technique, and some share common templates at the end of each section. Numerous quilt plans are provided. Also included in this section is a Glossary of Techniques that gives tips and instructions for all phases of quiltmaking.

Pieces of the Past has been a challenging project for me, full of new design possibilities. I hope you are challenged to incorporate these designs into your quiltmaking.

5

Linsey-Woolsey Quilt, origin unknown, c. 1800, 100" x 100". The backing was hand woven from handspun linen warp and wool weft, then home dyed a deep indigo. The linen top is quilted in leaf and laurel patterns and contains a wool filler. (Collection of Museum of History and Industry, Seattle, Washington)

Quilts in Colonial America 1750—1840

The scarcity of fabrics and textiles in colonial America challenged the ingenuity of the quiltmaker. Quilts required large amounts of fabric for the top, wool or cotton batting to be used as a filler, and a backing, usually of homespun fabric.

Textiles were one of the most valuable commodities in 18th-century America. England had kept her colonies dependent on her for textiles and fabrics, using America as a source for raw materials and discouraging the development of any textile production. The technology of England's textile machinery was carefully guarded. *Printed Textiles,* by Florence Montgomery, gives these figures on America's importation of fabrics: 90,616 yards in 1756; 353,762 yards in 1785, and 3,710,471 yards in 1800.

America's fabrics during this period, referred to as "homespun," were produced in homes on a small scale due to the time-consuming process involved. Wool had to be sheared from sheep, carded, and then spun into yarn before it was woven on a loom. Linen fabric was even more difficult to make, for the flax plant had to be broken into fibers or shreds before it could be spun and woven into linen cloth. Thus the early quilts were utility quilts, made more for a practical purpose than for their artistic beauty.

Several quilts have survived from this era and are referred to as "linsey-woolsey" quilts. (Linsey-woolsey is a sturdy material made from linen weft and wool warp.) These linsey-woolsey quilts usually consisted of a whole cloth top, which was home-dyed a deep tone, wool filler, and homespun backing. The solid color top was then embellished with decorative quilting, featuring feather plumes and wreaths, flowers, baskets, swags, and swirls.

Other surviving quilts from this period illustrate our reliance on England for both our fabrics and design styles. Broderie Perse was a popular style in England, as well as with wealthier colonial families. In Broderie Perse, figures were cut from English chintz (calico*) and then appliqued to background fabric. Indian chintzes with finely detailed figures suitable for Broderie Perse and Indian cottons were also popular in England.

Pieced and Applique Crib Quilt, Medallion/Broderie Perse, maker unknown, 1830-1840, New York, 34" x 33 1/2". Early printed cottons are combined with delicate chintz cutouts in this elegant miniature. Photograph from Thos. K. Woodard: American Antiques & Quilts courtesy E.P. Dutton, Inc. (Private collection)

*Calico is one of the oldest fabrics in the world. It was first made in India and exported by the British East India Company from the seaport of Calicut (today's Calcutta). This printed cotton cloth has been referred to as calico or chintz in England for more than 275 years.

Picced Child's Quilt, star, maker unknown, c. 1830, Connecticut, 60" x 58". This gem incorporates a sumptuous group of early printed cottons and chintzes. Photograph from Kelter-Malce Antiques courtesy E.P. Dutton, Inc. (Quilt now in private collection)

1. *Marie D. Webster, QUILTS: THEIR STORY AND HOW TO MAKE THEM, p. 60*

"The date of the quilt's advent into America is unknown, and—because of the lack of knowledge concerning the house furnishings of the early colonists—can never be positively determined. Quilts were in such general use and were considered as such ordinary articles that the early writers about family life in the colonies neglected to mention them. We do know, however, that quilted garments, bedspreads, curtains, and the like were very essential to the comfort and well-being of the original settlers along the Atlantic seaboard."[1]

Most of the printed cotton fabrics in colonial United States were imported from Europe and were available in large port cities such as Philadelphia and Baltimore. Wealthy city people could afford the early block- and copperplate printed fabrics, but farmers and pioneers far from fabric sources still relied on "homespun."

The dyeing of solid color cloth was practiced extensively in the home, and home-dyeing recipes were prevalent.

> Naturally, the pioneer woman knew she must "set the blue pot" in August when indigo was blooming. She learned, probably through trial and error, that "hick'ry bark'll make the lasting-est yeller," that madder root was an unfailing source, not only for pink but for that most popular of all quilt colors, Turkey red. Pokeberries produced lovely lavenders; walnut juice and butternut hulls were for making fast blacks and browns; cedar root made a royal purple, and cockleburr, "the prettiest of weeds," produced a rich deep gold. Gray was obtained from sumac with copperas, and descendants of the Scottish highlanders might remember that dandelion roots had been used to obtain a magenta for their tartans in the old days.[2]

> The lady of the house did not have to move far to gather supplies for her dye pot. They were practically at her doorstep, lily-of-the-valley or Queen Anne's lace for a delicate yellow, marigolds for a deep orange, hollyhocks for a good red, and, of course, there would be larkspur for blue as well as indigo. In her kitchen there were onion skins holding a potential for a deep rust color, and even spinach made a greenish yellow. But it was not as easy as just reaching out for the source. The following table is proof that it required large quantities to dye even one pound of wool:

> Barks - 1 peck finely chopped
> Leaves - 3/4 peck, dried
> Hulls - 1 peck
> Flowers - 1 1/2 quarts dried flower heads

Mistletoe contained a high green dye content, but it grew tall and was often inaccessible. The making of green remained the most baffling of all colors, being a combination of the two basic colors, blue and yellow.

It was time-consuming and the results were often disappointing. Little wonder that many of the old recipe books concluded with a philosophical bit of advice "just suit your fancy." That is why cloth made in such circumstances was something to be cherished.[3]

"What about the dyeing?" Clara asked.

"Ain't hard." Granny sounded a little smug. "Walnut and butternut hulls for browns and blacks. Pokeberries made lavender. Hic'kry bark makes the lastingest yeller ever ye seed. Madder's for red and pink, and—"

"But blue's best of all," Aunt Polly interrupted her. "Howsomever, we'd have t' put off 'till August to set the blue pot. Indigo don't bloom 'till then. My mamma had a blue pot that's in our barn yit."[4]

2. Lenice Bacon, *AMERICAN PATCHWORK QUILTS*, pp. 60—62.

3. Ibid.

4. Catherine Marshall, *CHRISTY*, p. 181.

In 1772 the first calico printworks in America was started in Kensington, Pennsylvania (near Philadelphia), with the help of Benjamin Franklin. As technology changed, so did the types of prints and colors available.

Block printing was used on fabric prior to the middle of the 18th century. This was a time-consuming process as the textile worker had to move the inked block from one area of material to another, being careful to line up or register the print. If other colors were to be used in the print, a separate inked block was used for each color, making the registration of the print even more difficult.

The copperplate printing process, invented in the mid-18th century, revolutionized fabric printing and made possible a wider variety of prints with greater detail. Since registration of detailed prints was still difficult, most of the plates were for one-color designs, such as blue or red, printed on a white background.

In 1783 Thomas Bell, a Scotsman, realized that copperplates could be curved around a roller; thus, it became possible to print lengths of fabric. However, these roller printed fabrics were not available to American quiltmakers until the early 1800s.[5]

By the end of the 1840's, a major transition had developed in the production of textiles. Although the homespun tradition continued in a minor way for decades, "advancements and innovations in machinery and dyes, notably the introduction of aniline dyes, made commercially produced printed-cotton textiles economically viable as a cheap replacement for home-produced textiles."[6]

The reliance on homespun materials and the shortage of quilting supplies in the more remote areas is reflected in the following quotes and interviews by John Rice Irwin in *A People and Their Quilts:*

Q. What did they use for the filler? Was it mostly cotton or wool?

A. Well, now just say you had some blankets or old quilts that was gettin' old and ragged. She'd put that between instead of batten. But she used cotton more'n anything. They's two pounds of cotton in every quilt she quilted. Two pounds of cotton will mean more than a feller thinks it will. She'd spin it and make the thread to weave the cloth—weave her lining. Then (she would) have to spin the thread to do the quilting with.

Q. The back of it would be hand spun?

A. Yeah, every bit of it.[7]

5. Barbara Brackman, "Dating Old Quilts, Part Two: Cotton Prints up to 1890," QUILTER'S NEWSLETTER MAGAZINE, Oct. 1984, p. 26.

6. Marilyn Kowalski, "Collectible Calicoes," COUNTRY LIVING MAGAZINE, March 1985, p. 61.

7. John Rice Irwin, A PEOPLE AND THEIR QUILTS, p. 118.

"Back then when I was first married we just used anything we could get to make quilts out of. Take men's clothes and cut the best out of them you know. They call them comforts—they're tacked in. Well they wasn't no pattern to them, just sew them in strips. They's awful thick—where they was made out of thick material. They'd tack them, and just called 'em comforts. They's heavy too. But them old heavy wool quilts felt good then, on a cold night."[8]

- Dolphia Elkins

"We'd take old worn-out pants, you know, and wash 'em and make quilts out of the best parts of them. Then my mother bought brown domestic sometimes. But she raised her own cotton and we'd pick it. She'd card the cotton for the quilt filling, and for spinning too. She'd card and I'd spin and weave it.

"We'd make towels out of cotton. We never had a store-bought towel all the time I's growing up. They were all made of old homemade stuff. And we had straw ticks and feather beds we slept on.

"Why, Mother never made no fancy patterns much. Most of her quilting was for old everyday quilts to keep you warm."[9]

- Clemmie Pugh

With the scarcity of fabrics and the difficulty of producing them at home, it is not surprising that the patchwork quilt evolved from these frugal colonial households. It appears that necessity was truly the "mother of invention" in the case of the patchwork quilt.

...life in the colonies was a challenge to the bravery and the ingenuity of the colonial housewife whose main concern was the welfare and survival of her family. Provisions for warmth were of utmost concern during the cold New England winters and when the clothing and quilts brought from Europe began to show signs of wear, she began to patch them together with scraps of fabric and the remains of clothing, until new ones could be made from fabrics brought from England. When even these haphazardly patched together quilts were too worn to keep anyone warm, they were used for the inner layers of new quilts, pieced together from the scraps after garments were cut from precious new cloth. The first new quilts made in America were most likely filled with grasses and corn husks and the layers held together with twine pulled through and tied in knots.[10]

Unaware, the frugal colonial housewife had begun a new art form, based on her long-time habits of thrift, practicality, and efficiency. These early quilts, composed of haphazard patches, slowly evolved into exquisite works of art, as each precious scrap of fabric was carefully cut and pieced into an overall geometric design.

8. Ibid., p. 105.

9. Ibid., p. 93.

10. Barbara Weiland, ed., NEEDLEWORK NOSTALGIA, p. 2.

11

Developing Designs

When studying early examples of quilts, we seem to find many patterns that developed along with piecing. Four-Patch, Ninepatch, Star of Lemoyne, Double Irish Chain, Variable Star, and Wild Goose Chase are generally simple, basic structures upon which today's quilt patterns are based. Many of these patterns developed in the period from 1750—1850.

Where did the inspiration for these quilting patterns come from? Many of the isolated cultures and early immigrants reused themes from their European heritage. These themes were passed down through the years and are still used on many varieties of their folk art.

A good example of these European themes being handed down came from the Germans who settled in Pennsylvania during the 1700's (wrongly referred to as the "Pennsylvania Dutch"). We see many of the same symbols repeated on their folk art. Pottery, quilts, stenciling, and scherenschnitte (the art of paper cutting) are decorated with vases of flowers and buds or overflowing urns and bowls, symbolizing abundance.

Another good example of a regional folk art pattern is the Southern Mammy quilt, sometimes called the Pickaninny quilt.* This pattern strongly reflects the African origin of the slaves in its primitive design. In Afro-American quilts, "largeness of design, rather than smallness, is aimed for because the overall effect is more important than intricate details. The individual pieces or the blocks may be large in scale because the quilts originally needed to be made quickly."[11]

As with most folk art, there was no early visual reference; patterns were passed down from person to person. This was especially true in the more isolated communities.

Pot of Flowers (detail), maker unknown, c. 1870, Pennsylvania. This was one of the symbols used by Pennsylvania Germans on their quilts, pottery, stenciling and other folk art. Photo courtesy E.P. Dutton, Inc. (Private collection)

Southern Mammy Quilt, by Nancy Martin, 1985, Woodinville, Washington, 28" x 28". (Collection of That Patchwork Place, Inc., Bothell, Washington.) Pattern available from Country House Quilts, 170 S. Main Street, Zionsville, IN 46077.

---

11. Roberta Horton, CALICO AND BEYOND: THE USE OF PATTERNED FABRIC IN QUILTS, p. 42.

*As with most folk art, the originator of this pattern is unknown, but variations of this design were found throughout the South.

During the early part of the 19th century, itinerant craftsmen and peddlers practiced their trades by traveling to the more isolated communities. Few cities were large enough to support the trade of a weaver, stenciler, or silhouette maker. (Common people, who could not afford to have a portrait painted, engaged the silhouette maker to make a likeness.) Frontier homes looked forward to the visit of an itinerant craftsman or peddler offering him hospitality and lodging for the night.

Detail: Princess Feather by Sarah Lhamon, 1861, Mt. Vernon, Ohio. The Princess Feather was a very popular pattern after 1850. Many examples of the design were made in the red and green fabrics then in fashion. The design can be traced to the feather crest of the English Prince of Wales and has been worked in quilting and crewel as well as in applique. This quilt is signed and dated in the center. (Collection of That Patchwork Place, Inc., Bothell, Washington)

The traveling peddler—were quilt patterns part of his stock in trade? In Johanna Bergen's Diary, kept on a Flatlands, Long Island, farm between 1824-1829, she says: "Peddler here today, took dinner with us, we made no trade with him." In the 1840's, in Pennsylvania, a peddler stayed overnight with one family; when the womenfolk deplored the fact they had no new quilt patterns with which to work, he asked for paper and scissors and proceeded to cut a design which, unfolded, revealed scrolls, leaves and complicated curlicues resembling those on old lacy valentines. From the pattern a quilt was made in dull yellow calico appliqued to a brown cambric background—it may be seen in the collection at Landis Valley Museum, Lancaster, Pennsylvania. Such itinerant salesmen discharged their debt for hospitality by carrying messages, gossip and news between farms and towns; alert to the needs of housewives, could they have been the carriers of the quilt patterns which appeared over so wide a radius of territory at approximately the same times?[12]

The isolated Appalachian mountain communities of today strongly reflect their English-Welsh background in their language and in their quilting motifs. The Prince of Wales feather-quilting design is a good example of a European motif continued in America.

Detail: Prince of Wales Feather quilting

It is interesting to note that patterns developed in blocks, a very functional and efficient approach to design. These pieced quilts, often utility quilts, could be made from salvaged scraps rather than purchasing the whole cloth.

The block-style method of quiltmaking is a time-saving device in which individual, identical blocks can be pieced one by one and later joined together. It is also space-saving, not a minor consideration given the cramped quarters of much early American rural living. Though larger homes followed as the colonies prospered, those who went to the frontier repeated the "huts and hovels" of early New England. The cabins they built were crowded with implements, children, bedding, cooking utensils, a few pieces of furniture, drying food, and the like. Blocks could be "lap-worked" one by one in contrast to the cumbersomeness of a progressively larger and larger fabric.[13]

12. Florence Peto, HISTORIC QUILTS, pp. 17.

13. Jonathan Holstein, THE PIECED QUILT, AN AMERICAN DESIGN TRADITION, P. 51.

Scrap, by Clara Countryman, c. 1880, Wyoming, Ohio, 79'' x 79''. An interesting collection of scraps, all different, are used in this one patch top. (Collection of Dick and Nancy Dice, Bellevue, Washington)

Double Ninepatch, origin unknown, c. 1900, 76 1/2'' x 89''. (Collection of That Patchwork Place, Inc., Bothell, Washington)

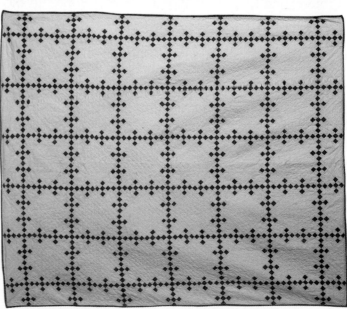

Nine Patch and Evening Stars, origin unknown, c. 1850, 44'' x 44''. Beautiful pattern and color make a very satisfying whole quilt. (Photograph from America Hurrah Antiques courtesy E.P. Dutton, Inc.)

Double Ninepatch Scrap, by Nancy Martin, 1985, Woodinville, Washington, 45 1/2'' x 64''. Deep colors and pieced lattices heighten the visual appeal of this quilt. Quilted by Andrea Scadden. (Collection of That Patchwork Place, Inc., Bothell, Washington)

Road to California, by Nancy Martin, 1985, Woodinville, Washington, 52" x 74". Quilted by Freda Smith. (Collection of That Patchwork Place, Inc., Bothell, Washington)

Pioneer Quilts 1840—1870

America was a country of eager and anxious settlers, always ready to establish new frontiers. Many young couples would gather their meager belongings and strike out on a long and perilous journey in search of their fortunes. Historians refer to this period as the "Western Movement," when our country established its doctrine of "Manifest Destiny."

These were hard and lonely years for pioneer women, who were removed from their families, friends, and fabric supplies. Quilts became a solace in their lives.

> It was during the years of the westward journey, from 1840 to 1870, that the majority of America's pieced quilts were stitched. As families moved west, fabric (though readily available in the East) once again became a scarce commodity. That scarcity led to the uniquely American patchwork masterpieces that have caught the world's eye and captured its heart...[14]

Old quilt patterns were carried west by the Pioneer women, and new ones were developed and named for the people, places, and events along the way. These patterns "reflected both the joys and sorrows of women's lives during pioneer times. Each one a work of art created out of the scrap bag, these quilts were stitched of geometric pieces painstakingly cut from cast-off clothing and tired household linens. Only on occasion were these precious scraps teamed with a new piece of cloth."[15]

Pioneer families moved many times, taking their treasured family quilts and Bibles with them. Many "everyday" quilts received years of hard use, keeping families warm in covered wagons or in unheated log cabins. But "best quilts" such as the Feathered Star bequeathed to Elizabeth Dearfield received special care.

14. Linda Joan Smith, "A Legacy of Quilts," COUNTRY HOME MAGAZINE, Feb. 1986, p. 67.

15. Ibid.

Detail: Feathered Star by Nancy Martin Dearfield, c. 1847, Pleasants County, West Virginia. Worked in red chintz and muslin, this quilt is typical of many Feathered Star quilts made in the 1800s. Shown with Dearfield family Bible. (Collection of That Patchwork Place, Inc., Bothell, Washington)

The Feathered Star quilt pictured here was made by Nancy Martin Dearfield, born 5 March 1827 and deceased 6 September 1914. The Martin family resided in southwestern Pennsylvania. Nancy Martin married Orlander Stephens Dearfield in Pleasants County, West Virginia. (The two areas are about 50 miles apart.) The Dearfields had three sons: Oliver born in 1861, Orlander born in 1863, and William born in 1868, all of whom moved west at varying times.

Nancy and Orlander Dearfield moved many times during the ensuing years: first to Lancaster County, Nebraska, then to join "Brother William" in southern Idaho, and then to Corvallis, Oregon. Nancy Martin Dearfield left the Feathered Star quilt to her granddaughter, Elizabeth, upon her death. Elizabeth was only seven years old at the time.

Patricia Mainardi in *Quilts, The Great American Art,* comments on the care given to these "best" quilts:

Moreover, the women who made quilts knew and valued what they were doing: frequently quilts were signed and dated by the maker, listed in her will with specific instructions as to who should inherit them, and treated with all the care that a fine piece of art deserves. Women reserved their "best" quilt for guests of honor or special occasions, and when it was on the bed drew the curtains to prevent fading. Many of the most beautiful quilts were actually used so infrequently that they have come down to us without ever having been laundered. Women even made special "quilt cases" to store them in. Even in their choice of material, women quiltmakers behaved similarly to other artists. They wanted to use only the most permanent materials, and the popularity of two colors, indigo and turkey red (an alizarin dye), was the result of their ability to withstand much use without fading.[16]

Feathered Star by Nancy Martin Dearfield, c. 1847, Pleasants County, West Virginia, 81" x 93". (Collection of That Patchwork Place, Inc., Bothell, Washington)

16. *Patricia Mainardi, QUILTS THE GREAT AMERICAN ART, p. 6.*

Log Cabin, origin unknown, c. 1860-1870, 74" x 74". Log Cabin blocks made from richly detailed fabrics are set in a "pinwheel" pattern. The quilt has a homespun backing. (Collection of Jan Halgrimson, Edmonds, Washington)

Bear's Paw, by Nancy Martin, 1984, Woodinville, Washington, 66" x 66". Both the Bear's Paw block and Sawtooth border reflect the pioneer influence on quilt names. (Collection of That Patchwork Place, Inc., Bothell, Washington)

Pioneer life and its daily struggles also contributed names to the many quilt block patterns that evolved. The most notable is the Log Cabin design which dates from the mid-1800s. This design is assembled in much the same manner as a log cabin. Its central red block, signifing the chimney of the cabin, comes first. Then two sides, opposite each other, are added, followed by the other two sides, and so on. And just as the log cabin is affixed to a foundation of stones, the Log Cabin block is worked on a foundation of muslin fabric.

The Log Cabin is one of the most symbolic and popular quilt patterns. The man of the family protected his family from the elements in an unknown land as they journeyed westward. And at the end of their journey, he used his axe to provide an immediate shelter—the log cabin. The Log Cabin block became a visual symbol for the self-reliance and self-sufficiency of the American pioneers.

18

Bear's Paw, The Anvil, Barn Raising, Indian Hatchet, Chips and Whetstone, and the many Sawtooth Stars and Sawtooth borders reflect this pioneer influence on quilt designs.

In *A People and Their Quilts,* John Rice Irwin comments on the origin of the name Chips and Whetstone:

> "The Whetstone was carried by the man of the house to sharpen his axe; for he was always chopping trees. Hundreds of times I have seen my grandfather sharpen his axe with his whetstone, then lay it beside a stump amidst piles of chips from the recently cut tree.
>
> "I don't know whether or not this type of wetrock, and these type of chips, are connected with the derivation of the quilt's name, but that's what I think of when I hear the name, Chips and Whetstone. The eight points of the star represent the whetstones, and the small pieces surrounding them are the chips: fresh-scented ash, oak, and hickory chips."[17]

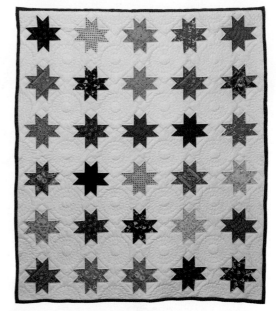

Sawtooth Star, by Pam Reising, 1984, Cincinnati, Ohio, 42 1/2" x 51". (Collection of Comforts of Home, Cincinnati, Ohio)

Chips and Whetstone, quilt top by Emma Mittendorf, c. 1870, 92" x 92". The Chips and Whetstone blocks were pieced from old fabrics just after the Civil War by Emma Mittendorf. They were later set together with pastel fabrics by Clara Walker around 1930. (Collection of Sylvia and Jack Mittendorf, Seattle, Washington)

17. Irwin, A PEOPLE AND THEIR QUILTS, p. 78.

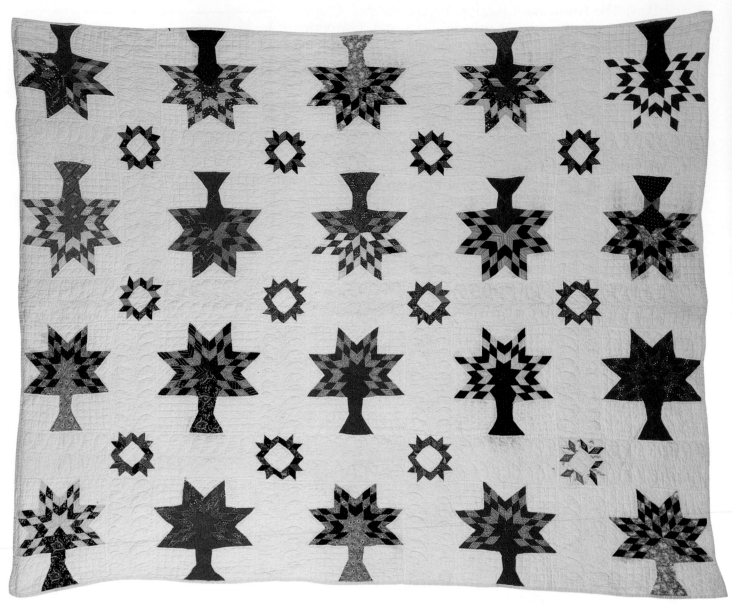

Peony Tree, origin unknown, c. 1890, 73 1/2'' x 86 1/2''. (Collection of Toni Flink, Seattle, Washington)

Calico Craze 1850—1890

After colorfast dyes were invented in 1856, a wide variety of prints became available and affordable. By this time Cranston Printworks could print almost a million and a half yards of calico per week. These calicoes contained detailed figures on finely drawn backgrounds with minute shading and texture (dots and tiny lines).

Blue was the earliest fast dye and a popular color for patchwork quilts. Blue and white quilts were popular during the 1800s, and those made at the beginning of the century were hand dyed using the indigo plant.

During the 1870s and 1880s, florals and geometrics, as well as sports prints, were popular. Sports prints with tennis rackets, riding whips, bows and arrows, cars, and horseshoes were a fad. Detailed prints of thimbles, pins, needles, and thread were also common. Women used these fabrics to design quilts and several recurring themes emerged during this period.

Navigation and the Sea

As cities on the Eastern Seaboard grew in mercantile trade, women living there designed quilt blocks reflecting America's dependence on sea commerce. Blocks containing clipper ships appear on several of the Baltimore album quilts. Mariner's Compass and Ocean Waves were popular quilt block patterns using the sea as a design theme.

Ocean Waves, Griffith family quilt, c. 1890, New York, 72" x 85". A wonderful collection of turn of the century fabric scraps surrounds the pink centers of the Ocean Waves quilt. (Collection of Robert and Marian Griffith, Edmonds, Washington)

Mariner's Star, by Jane Scott, 1840, 76" x 82". This pieced and appliqued quilt has the maker's name and date among the heavy quilting. (Collection of Museum of History and Industry, Seattle, Washington)

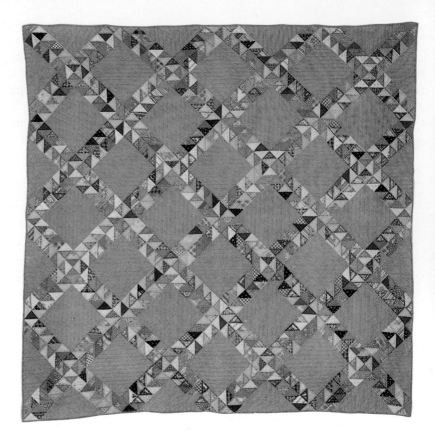

Lady of the Lake, Griffith family quilt, c. 1890, New York, 76" x 76". Sir Walter Scott's epic poem inspired the name of this block. (Collection of Dotty Charlson, Edmonds, Washington)

Literature

Popular literature of the day also influenced quilt themes. "Lady of the Lake," Sir Walter Scott's epic poem (published in 1810) in which he wrote about the tales and traditions of Scotland's loch country, was especially interesting to pioneer men and women. By naming a quilt block, Lady of the Lake, "women honored the author in their most practical form of artistic expression. This is one of the few patterns which has never been known by any other name."[18]

Pilgrim's Progress was written by John Bunyan in 1675, while the author was imprisoned for preaching the Gospel without official sanction. Throughout the next two centuries it was printed and read more often than any other book except the Bible. The book was written for the common people, most of whom neither owned nor read many books. The goal of the characters were the Delectable Mountains, symbols of peace and plenty in the new land of evergreens.

"...the Delectable Mountains...and behold at a great distance he saw a most pleasant, Mountainous Country, beautified with Woods, Vineyards, Fruits of all sorts, Flowers also, with Springs and Fountains, very delectable to behold."[19]

Delectable Mountains by Lois Odell, 1984, Kirkland, Washington, 54" x 54". This green and white wall quilt embodies the feelings of peace and plenty expressed in John Bunyan's description of the evergreen-covered new land in **Pilgrim's Progress.** The book was written in the 1600s, and the name Delectable Mountains was adopted early as a quilt pattern name in this country. (Collection of the artist)

18. *Ruth E. Finley, OLD PATCHWORK QUILTS AND THE WOMEN WHO MADE THEM, p. 76.*

19. *John Bunyan, PILGRIM'S PROGRESS, p. 72.*

Patriotism

Patriotism was, and continues to be, a popular theme in folk art as well as quilts. The eagle, a symbol of liberty and our heritage, has long been used in quilt designs.

Patriotism emerged as a design theme in the many quilts that were made for America's Centennial and Bicentennial. Patriotic quilts were again created in 1985 for the Great American Quilt Festival, celebrating the Statue of Liberty Centennial. Red, white, and blue color schemes were prominent in all of these quilts.

"A quilt festival," states Dr. Robert Bishop, director of the Museum of American Folk Art, "is particularly appropriate as a tribute to the Statue of Liberty—that most symbolic of American icons. Quilts play such an important part in the lives of the American people. They are priceless documents of America's heritage, lovingly and thoughtfully created. Enthusiasm for them is shared by art lovers, antique collectors, and millions of quiltmakers."

Out of Many, One, by Judy Eide, 1985, Woodinville, Washington, 72" x 72". The maker explains the symbolism used in this quilt made for the Great American Quilt Festival Contest celebrating the Statue of Liberty Centennial, "Men, women, and children of all ages and races come from all over the world to this country in pursuit of liberty; all help to keep the flame alive as a priceless gift to pass on to our children and grandchildren. This concept is framed within a diamond (itself a symbol of priceless value) and guarded by four bald eagles, symbols of America. The large stars represent each of the geographic areas (50 states, Washington D.C., and foreign military bases and territories) participating in the contest. The smaller stars represent us as individual citizens." (Collection of the artist)

54-40 or Fight, by Marsha McCloskey, 1986, Seattle, Washington, 39" x 49". (Collection of the artist)

Political Views

Quilts also provided an outlet for women to express their political opinions, since they did not receive the vote until 1920. Up until this point, women were not to have political opinions or preferences, since that fell into the public sphere of family life for which the man was in charge.

Many quilt blocks are named for political figures or political events: Whig Rose, Radical Rose, Clay's Choice, Harrison Rose, Burgoyne Surrounded. Some of these quilt blocks were designed as a woman's statement of her feeling at the time of the event, such as making a Radical Rose block with a black center to show her sympathy for the abolitionist movement or a Whig Rose quilt expressing preference for the Whig party.

The quilt block 54-40-or Fight was named for the dispute over the northern boundary of the United States. Both the British, in the form of the Hudson's Bay Company, and the United States had established settlements in the Northwest. They agreed to a treaty in 1818, allowing joint occupancy of the territory. However, a bitter dispute over the boundary arose in 1844, and that became the rallying cry of the United States presidential campaign. The numbers refer to the degree of latitude which the Americans wished to establish as the northern boundary. In 1846 a treaty was signed, which set the present northern boundary.

Clay's Choice was named for the popular American statesman, Henry Clay. In 1839 Henry Clay gave a speech in which he declared himself against slavery. He stated that the abolitionists were responsible for the quarrels that were threatening to break up the nation. Clay's friends warned him that his speech would ruin his chance to become president of the United States. He then remarked, "I would rather be right, than President." Unfortunately, Henry Clay got his wish.

Clay's Choice, by Marsha McCloskey, 1986, Seattle, Washington, 36" x 48". (Collection of the artist)

However, many blocks having political or historical names were designed to commemorate an event after it happened, as noted quilt historian Barbara Brackman relates.

Burgoyne Surrounded is the popular name for the design which is nearly identical to a weaving pattern used in making overshot coverlets. That quilt pattern is usually said to be the work of a patriotic seamstress during the American Revolution who commemorated the victory of the colonial soldiers against the British General John Burgoyne by adapting the battle plan to a quilt design. Stories like this are one of the reasons quilts capture our imagination but, unfortunately, most of the stories are based purely on imagination.

Looking through my library of quilt books for old quilts made using that pattern, I found no evidence that the design goes back to the Revolutionary War. I found several 19th century examples; dated 1852 and 1859; and there were four others attributed to the years 1850—1875, but none earlier than mid-19th century—75 years after General Burgoyne was defeated. More likely the pattern was generated mid-19th century, copied from the overshot coverlet design.[20]

Burgoyne Surrounded, by Donna Hanson Eines, Edmonds, Washington, 1985, 84" x 101". Stunning quilting and a striking pieced border enhance this design from the mid-19th century. (Collection of the artist)

20. Barbara Brackman, "Patterns to Ponder," *QUILTWORLD OMNIBOOK, Winter 1985, p. 6.*

25

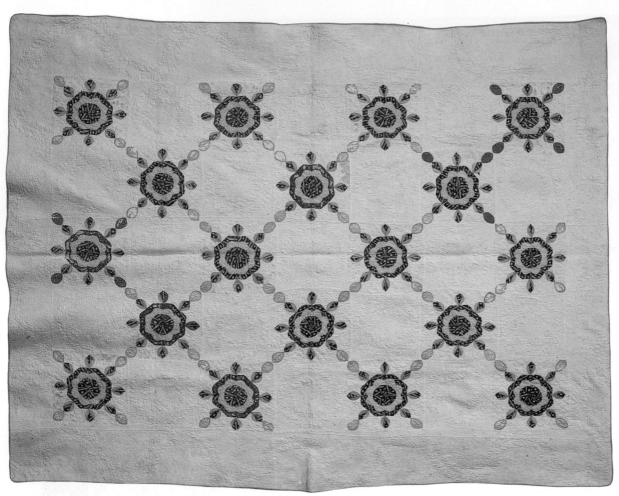

Whig Rose, by Addie Shinn, c. 1847, 70" x 90". This variation of the Whig Rose pattern is quilted with a feathered wreath design. The Whig Rose quilt was often made by a quiltmaker to express her preference for the Whig Party. (Collection of Museum of History and Industry, Seattle, Washington)

Detail: Temperance Tree, origin unknown c. 1900. (Collection of That Patchwork Place, Inc., Bothell, Washington)

21. *Geraldine P. Morse to Esther White, n.d.*

22. *Barbara Brackman, "Patterns to Ponder," QUILTWORLD OMNIBOOK, Summer 1985, p. 6.*

Some quilts had a more direct effect on political events. Many quilts were made as raffle quilts to help support the campaign of a favored political leader. Others served as symbols of freedom for escaping slaves, as part of the Underground Railroad.

During the Civil War, red dye was not available, so black was used in the hearth blocks (centers of the Log Cabin blocks). These Log Cabin quilts with black hearth blocks were hung on the line to indicate an Underground Railroad stop.[21]

Raffle quilts were also made to support the Temperance Movement. The Women's Christian Temperance Union block had a strip across the center for a signature. The privilege of signing the quilt could be purchased for a dime or a quarter. Other quilt blocks associated with the Temperance Movement were Drunkard's Path and Capital T.

During the last half of the 19th century and the early part of this century, many women directed their political and moral energies to the Temperance Movement. Temperance Tree was first printed in the Ohio Farmer in 1894, it goes back at least to 1876 when a letter writer mentioned making a Temperance Tree quilt, possibly to show her support of the movement.[22]

Tree of Life, by Nancy Martin, 1986, Woodinville, Washington, 74" x 74". (Collection of That Patchwork Place, Inc., Bothell, Washington)

Religious Inspiration

It is not unusual that women used the subject matter of their lives as a design inspiration for their quilts. Many quilt blocks were inspired by religion or the Bible, both of which were central in the lives of the first settlers. America was founded on the principle of religious freedom, and our ancestors demonstrated their faith daily. The church provided some of the few social gatherings for which the busy housewife could allot time.

Although most quilts with religious themes tended to be "best quilts" done in applique or featuring exquisite quilting, many scrap quilts also were made from those patterns.

Jacob's Ladder quilt top, made by Clara Countryman, 1935, Wyoming, Ohio, 69 1/2" x 78 1/2". Made for the birth of her grandson, Dick Dice. (Collection of Dick and Nancy Dice, Bellevue, Washington)

Caesar's Crown, origin unknown, 74" x 96". (Collection of That Patchwork Place, Inc., Bothell, Washington)

Render therefore under Caesar the things which are Caesar's; and unto God the things that are God's. Matt. 22:21

Quilting designs also were used to depict Christian or religious symbols. Elly Sienkiewicz, in *Spoken without a Word,* identifies and interprets these symbols:

The Fleur de Lis is a symbol for the Trinity and the Virgin Mary in Christian Iconography; and for the Flame of Light, Life and Power in the French national emblem. Spiritually significant grapes, cherries, and strawberries are the fruits most often featured as wreaths. The grape vine symbolizes Christ and the Church; cherry clusters denote Sweet Character and Good Works (cherry twins means Love's Charm); a strawberry trefoil means the Christian Trinity, while strawberries in general are symbols for Esteem and Love, their leaves meaning Completion or Perfection.

To add a few additional often-used blocks, but by no means completing the list, there are crossed oak branches, and oaks in wreaths and sprays, even acorns and oak leaves in a cornucopia! These mean respectively: Victory; Courage; Longevity; Immortality; the oak tree itself standing for Hospitality, Stability, Strength of Faith and Virtue; symbol of the Christian's Strength Against Adversity.[23]

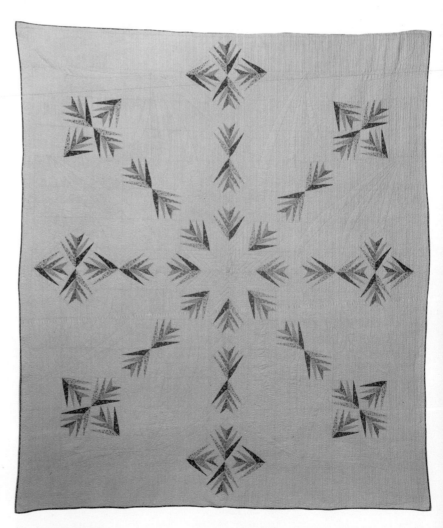

Hosannah (The Palms), origin unknown, c. 1920, 78" x 94". A deeply religious woman from Maine created The Palms pattern, inspired by the Bible story of Christ's triumphant entry into Jerusalem. (Collection of The Stearns and Foster Company, Cincinnati, Ohio)

When they heard that Jesus was coming to Jerusalem, they took branches of palm trees, and went forth to meet him, and cried, Hosannah! Blessed is the King of Israel that cometh in the name of the Lord. John 12:12-13

---

23. Elly Sienkiewicz, *SPOKEN WITHOUT A WORD,* p. 21.

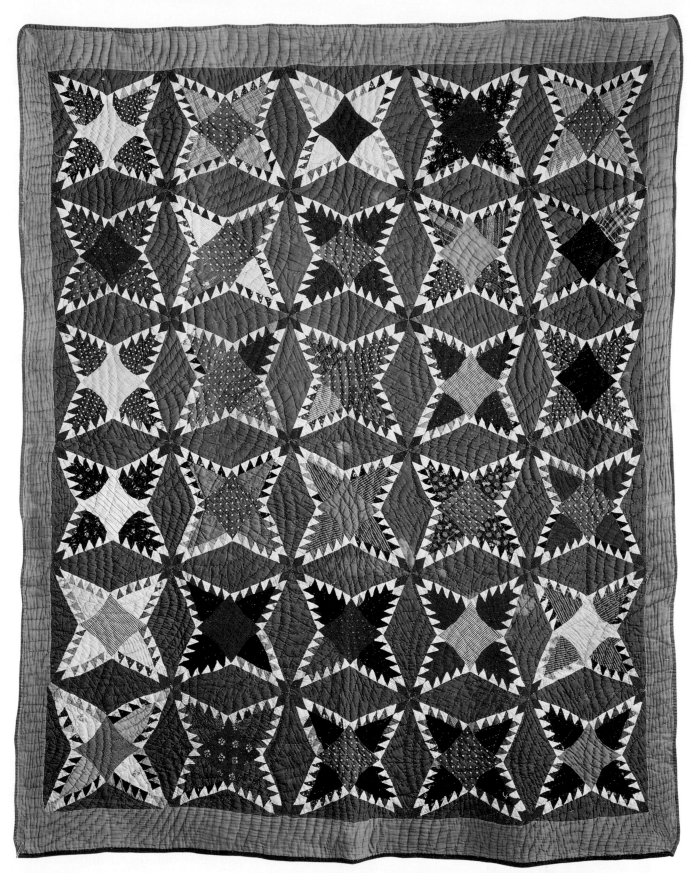

Feathered World Without End, maker unknown, c. 1900, Pennsylvania, 84" x 66". Unusual colors, bold graphics and a warm heavy texture make this a splendid country quilt. (Photograph from Kelter-Malce Antiques courtesy E.P. Dutton, Inc.)

Glory be to the Father, and to the Son, and to the Holy Ghost, as it was in the Beginning, it is now and ever shall be, world without end. Amen. Book of Common Prayer

Detail: Rose of Sharon block, Rose Burkette, Bothell, Washington

Detail: Rose of Sharon block, Marjorie Meyers, Bothell, Washington

Detail: Rose of Sharon block, Nancyann Johanson Twelker, Seattle, Washington.

Detail: Rose of Sharon block, Nancy Martin, Woodinville, Washington

Ruth Finley, in *Old Patchwork Quilts and the Women Who Made Them,* provides us with an insight into the women who made quilts based on Biblical themes. Her interpretation is more passionate than one might expect.

>...Here again the staid needlewomen of the eighteenth century went to the Bible for a name, finding it in the most passionately exalted love lyric of all time, ''The Song of Songs Which is Solomon's''.
>
> In the King James version the Shulamite princess's great opening soliloquy is divided into three chapters, but it reads as one paean of triumphant love glorying in surrender:
>
> Let him kiss me with the kisses of his mouth
> For thy love is better than wine.
>
> ....
> I am the Rose of Sharon
> And the lily of the valleys.
> As the lily among the thorns
> So is my love among the daughters;
> As the apple tree among the trees of the wood
> So is my beloved among the sons.
> His left hand is under my head—
> His right hand doth embrace me.
>
> ....
> My beloved is mine and I am his—
> He feedeth among the lilies.

The accepted tradition of early American womanhood is one of inarticulate, suppressed emotions. Austere, efficient, kind but cold, have our grandmothers been labeled. But it takes only a little delving into the life of the times, only a little reading between the lines of yellowed letters and diaries, only a little interpretation of ways that now seem merely quaint, to reveal depths of tenderness and heights of feeling.

...These women of a by-gone generation who knew so well the difference between sentiment and sentimentality named their most frequently reproduced, and one of their oldest, appliqued quilt patterns ''The Rose of Sharon''. Incidentally, it was almost invariably a bride's quilt, being the most often used of all applique patterns for that final touch to the dowry. And so the name surely was chosen, not only for its own poetic beauty, but also out of an appreciative understanding of the age-old poem which recounts the story of the very human love of a man and a woman.[24]

24. *Finley, OLD PATCHWORK QUILTS, p. 126.*

Domestic Tranquility

Yet it was women's domestic life which contributed the names of most of the quilt patterns. Churn Dash, Goose in the Pond, Corn and Beans, Hole in the Barn Door are names that reflect farm life, which is not surprising, since, up until 1920, most people lived on farms; only 2 percent of our population resided in cities. Other quilt names reflect events or objects in women's busy domestic routines: Basket, Birds in the Air, Broken Dishes, Cake Stand, Cut Glass Dish, Hovering Hawks, Pickle Dish, Pineapple, Puss in a Corner, Setting Sun, Spider Web, Waterwheel, Weathervane, and Whirlygig.

The woman of the family was responsible for all the domestic chores (cooking, clothing, gardening), in addition to caring for her large family. (The average woman in 1800 had 7.6 children.) These were tremendously difficult tasks, especially since canned goods were not available until 1850; and, before the advent of refrigeration, all meat for winter meals had to be slaughtered, smoked, salted, or cured. Laundry was so time-consuming that standards of cleanliness were less than those today.

Women also had the job of producing bedcovers for their large families—not an easy task since homes were unheated during the night. (Not many blankets were available for purchase before 1860.) Many of the quilts produced were utility quilts, quickly tacked together for their warmth.

Bow Tie, made by Lulu V. McCurdy, c. 1930, Tacoma, Washington, 67'' x 78''. Made from scraps for the youth bed of Peter Johanson. (Collection of Nancyann Twelker, Seattle, Washington)

Double Wedding Ring, made by Florence Wells Watson, c. 1940, Sumas, Washington, 65'' x 78''. An interesting variation of the Double Wedding Ring pattern done in vibrant fabrics. (Collection of Suzanne Hammond, Bellingham, Washington)

Pickle Dish, origin unknown, c. 1900, 72'' x 72''. (Collection of Peg Storey, Seattle, Washington)

Log Cabin, Sunshine and Shadow Variation, maker unknown, c. 1900, New England, 73 1/2'' x 74 1/2''. (Collection of Carol Harker, Bothell, Washington)

Spider Web quilt top, Mittendorf family quilt, c. 1930, Pennsylvania, 73'' x 73''. (Collection of Rosalie Pfeifer, Kent, Washington)

Cake Stand, origin unknown, c. 1890, 85'' x 75''. Scarcity of fabrics resulted in irregular sizes of many old quilts. Here the unknown quiltmaker saved her intricate pieced border for the visible sides of the quilt. A double row of stitches, a favorite quilting design of the Amish, is used on this charming quilt. (Collection of That Patchwork Place, Inc., Bothell, Washington)

Basket, made by Nancy Martin and friends, Woodinville, Washington, 1985, 42'' x 54''. (Collection of That Patchwork Place, Inc., Bothell, Washington)

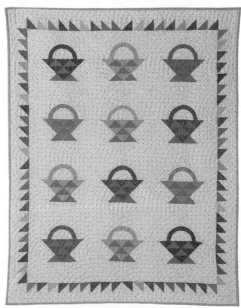

32

Cut Glass Dish, made by Nancy Martin, 1986, Seattle, Washington, 84'' x 84''. Cut Glass Dish blocks pieced from scrap fabrics are used in a "barnraising set". Pink and green color combinations were popular from the last quarter of the 19th century until the 1920s when pastel color schemes were favored. (Collection of That Patchwork Place, Inc., Bothell, Washington)

Goose in the Pond by Marsha McCloskey, 1985, Seattle, Washington, 60'' x 60''. Ruby McKim called Goose in the Pond "one of those homey old-fashioned names that grace so many patchworks". (Collection of the artist)

A quote from Flossie Cornett in John Rice Irwin's *A People and Their Quilts* illustrates the reliance on tacked quilts:

"I started helping my mother quilt when I was 8 years old, and she died when I was 11. They was ten of us children and it took a lot of bed covers to keep warm. We tacked them—we didn't quilt them for the kids. Now, my mother made some nice quilts, but they was for company. My mother made nice quilts."[25]

It is interesting to examine the "dry goods" pages from the early Sears Catalogs. For women who lived in remote areas away from larger cities, this catalog was their main resource for all the fabric they used: fabric for clothing, sheets, pillowcases, bed ticking, and quilts.[26]

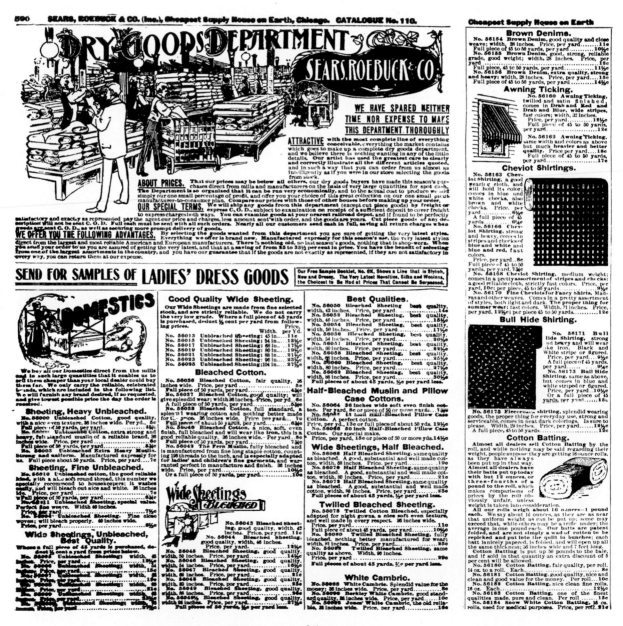

Women accepted their many domestic chores as part of the ideology of "womanhood." Nineteenth-century ladies were to be pious, pure, domestic, and submissive. These virtues were extolled by all who influenced their lives: the weekly sermons of their ministers, articles and novels from *Godey's Lady's Book,* and popular etiquette books. The man of the family was to take care of the public sphere of their lives, while the woman was to stay at home inside her domestic sphere.

Since women were expected to function only in the domestic sphere, their need for formal education was denied. Most young girls attended only a few years of grammar school before they were needed to help with the many chores at home.

Young ladies from wealthier families were privileged to attend academies, where they were educated in utilitarian art and needlework for their homes. They were taught needlework, tatting, lacemaking, wax bouquets, china painting, and other ornamental arts, which were intended to comfort their families. The purpose of this teaching was to instill the young ladies with a sense of industry, repetition, and self-discipline. Most of these detailed items were produced before marriage, for after marriage their time for needlework diminished, and often their eyesight was too poor when time became available after the child-raising period.

Needlework was not confining to all women, and there were many positive aspects to this domestic endeavor. Needlework was one of the few outlets of creative expression available at that time, since women were not allowed to participate in art education.

> Women have always made art. But for most women, the arts highest valued by male society have been closed to them for just that reason. They have put their creativity instead into the needlework arts, which exist in fantastic variety wherever there are women, and which in fact are a universal female art, transcending race, class and national borders. Needlework is the one art in which women controlled the education of their daughters, the production of the art, and were also the audience and critics...[27]

Broken Dishes, made by Nancy Martin, 1984, Bothell, Washington, 34" x 34". Made from old quilt blocks. Quilted by Freda Smith. (Collection of That Patchwork Place, Inc., Bothell, Washington)

Spider Web quilt top, made by Marsha McCloskey, 1985, Seattle, Washington, 32" x 32". (Collection of the artist)

25. Irwin, *A PEOPLE AND THEIR QUILTS, p. 99.*

26. *Sears Roebuck and Company Catalog, Fall 1900, p. 590—91.*

27. *Mainardi, QUILTS, THE GREAT AMERICAN ART, pp. 1—2.*

Sunflower, origin unknown, c. 1850, 72'' x 74''. This scrap quilt boasts a wonderful assortment of old fabrics. (Collection of Museum of History and Industry, Seattle, Washington)

Weathervane, made by Nancy Martin, 1985, Woodinville, Washington, 70'' x 70''. Farm objects inspired the names of many quilt blocks. Detailed quilting and feather wreaths by Andrea Scadden. (Collection of That Patchwork Place, Inc., Bothell, Washington)

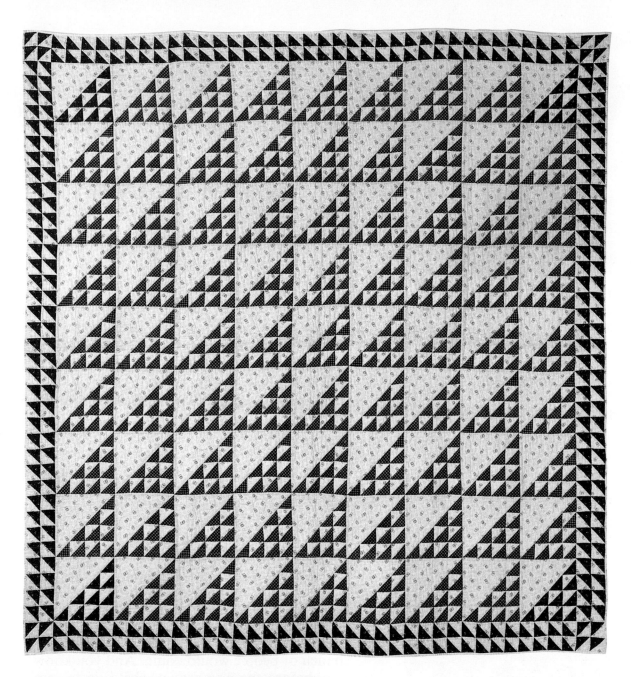

Birds in the Air, Griffith family quilt, c. 1890, New York, 73" x 74". A magnificent pieced quilt using a variety of indigo blue prints. Indigo and white quilts were popular during the 1800s. (Collection of Robert and Marian Griffith, Edmonds, Washington)

Puss in a Corner, made by Nancy Martin, 1985, Woodinville, Washington, 74" x 74". Quilted by Judy Eide. (Collection of That Patchwork Place, Inc., Bothell, Washington)

Hovering Hawks, made by Marsha McCloskey, 1985, Seattle, Washington, 30" x 30", (Collection of the artist)

Pickle Dish, origin unknown, c. 1900, 72" x 72". This wonderful overall design, executed in scraps, is quilted with the Baptist Fan pattern. (Collection of Peg Storey, Seattle, Washington)

28. *Ibid., p. 3.*

29. *"Denver Art Museum Quilt Collection," DENVER ART MUSEUM QUARTERLY, Winter 1963, p. 7.*

30. *Irwin, A PEOPLE AND THEIR QUILTS, p. 88.*

31. *Ibid., p. 23.*

Quiltmaking was also a way to achieve fame and emerge from the anonymity of domestic routine.

Although quilts had a functional purpose as bed coverings, they had another purpose equally important to their makers, and that is display. Early bedrooms frequently possessed only one piece of furniture, namely the bed, and the quilt displayed on the bed was the central motif. Women exhibited their quilts, and still do, at state and county fairs, churches and grange halls, much as our contemporary "fine" art is exhibited in museums and with much the same results. Good quilt makers were known and envied throughout their area, the exhibition of exceptionally fine craftswomanship and design influenced other women who returned home stimulated to do even finer work...[28]

The importance of quilts in women's lives was best expressed in the statement of one 19th-century farm woman, Lydia Roberts Dunham, who was quoted as saying, "I would have lost my mind if I had not had my quilts."[29]

Besides having a calming, soothing, and therapeutic effect on women, quilting had the potential to end women's isolation. Women engaged in few social activities, but a quilting bee, where neighbors were invited to help finish the quilt, was a legitimate excuse for socializing. Quotes from John Rice Irwin's *A People and Their Quilts* tell of quilting bees:

"You asked me about quilting parties. If we had room enough, we'd put up three quilts at a time and really have a big one. I told Fannie the other day that if she'd have a quiltin' show, she'd have room for four. (Mary laughs.) Yeah, a whole bunch of people would come. And you know, Fannie, before she was grown, she'd go to 'em. And she took the brag name of being the nicest quilter. Made the little stitches."[30]

- Mary Cross

Quilting bees often involved a community endeavor to make a present for one of its members. The church members made quilts for their preacher. Quilts were made for a young lady of the community as a wedding present, and the girls and young women made quilts for the young men in their community. These were sometimes signed by the girls and were known as Friendship quilts. Many quilting bees were held to make a quilt for the family in whose home it was "set up." Diaries, letters and other documents report a woman "putting up a quilt" and then inviting her neighbors.[31]

- John Rice Irwin

Samplers, stitched versions of the alphabet or verses, were a hallmark of a young lady's accomplishment and a sign of affluence. A family was considered poor if they didn't have a sampler to hang in the parlor. Since samplers were made in school, they demonstrated that a family could afford a proper education for a daughter.

Formal education for women was far more widespread than historians generally recognize. Girls, like boys, attended school only when they could be spared from household chores or factory work, and were instructed in basic reading and arithmetic. A girl was considered educated once she could read the New England Primer and needlework was considered her most important subject.

Samplers had a practical use in the school curriculum. Girls attended dame schools or nursery schools from age three to eight where they would work alphabet and numeral samplers in silk on linen. These simple samplers served a dual purpose: helping girls learn their letters and numbers and teaching the necessary skill of marking fine household linen with cross-stitch.

Girls graduated from basic samplers to art pieces with verses, pictures, and borders. These skills were taught in both local academies and boarding schools run by a talented needlewoman. Silk was used only by the advanced students since a misstitch could not be removed. When a daughter brought home her needlework, it was exhibited with pride. However, originality of design was not encouraged, thus the sampler represented the artistry of the teacher.[32]

Mothers, not teachers, passed their quilting skills to their daughters. Many women tell of fond memories of their mother quilting. Carolann Palmer remembers:

"My earliest recollection of quilting is the quilt frame filling up the entire room—it was a small dining room—at our home in Newberg, Oregon. The ladies of the community, I think they were called the Stitch and Chatter Club, were sitting around the frame. I remember how neat it was when I was tall enough to walk around and feel the quilt touch my head. For several weeks at a time the rest of the family had to walk around the dining room by going through the hall, because the quilt frame and quilters occupied the entire room. I got to go under the quilt!

I used to beg my mother, a few years later, not to sew the pieces together until I got home from school. I used to sit cross-legged on the floor near the treadle and cut the chains (cut the pieces apart). She used to beg me not to go so fast—'slow down, she'd say.'

Detail: Sampler verse stitched in hand dyed silk thread:

Jesus permit thy gracious name to stand
At the first effort of an infant hand
And while her fingers o'er this canvas move
Engage her tender heart to seek thy love
With thy dear children let her share a part
And write thy name thyself upon her heart
Rachel Jackson her Work Wrought in
the 13 Year of her age 1822
(Collection of Cherry Jarvis, Woodinville, Washington)

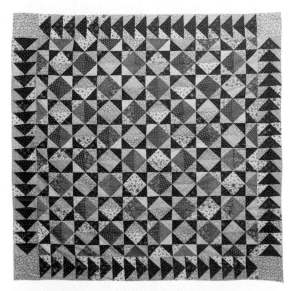

Variable Star, made by Carolann Palmer, 1986, Seattle, Washington, 66" x 66". (Collection of the artist)

32. Faudry, Marguerite and Deborah Brown, *THE BOOK OF SAMPLERS*, p. 62.

"My mother learnt me to quilt when I's just a young child. We'd work in the fields and gardens and when it was cold or rainy, we'd quilt, or spin and weave. [33]

— Clemmie Pugh

Burgoyne Surrounded, 79" x 94", made by Nancy Siler, c. 1890, Palouse, Washington. (Collection of Carolann Palmer, Seattle, Washington)

Lone Star, made by Nancy Siler, c. 1900, Palouse, Washington, 82" x 82". (Collection of That Patchwork Place, Inc., Bothell, Washington)

Carpenter's Wheel blocks, origin unknown, c. 1870. (Collection of Rosalie Pfeifer, Kent, Washington)

But not all daughters' recollections of quilting mothers are so pleasant. Perhaps the stress of so many moves and the daily farm chores produced erratic behavior in Nancy Siler. Her daughter Gladine Siler tells us that her mother was born Nancy Jane Clark on 25 November 1855 in Sullivan, Illinois. She married William Siler in 1874. Gladine records the moves the family made and adds these comments:

Move to Carralton, Missouri 1875; to Portland, Oregon by train then to Albany, Oregon by wagon 1877; Scio, Oregon 1882; Camp Creek 1884; and then to Palouse, Washington 1900 or 1901.

Nancy had nine children. Farm life left little time to quilt. She raised her children to do a lot of the house and farm work. She had one "joy" in life, quilting. During her second or third month of pregnancy, she went to bed and had her children wait on her. When her husband was gone all day in the fields, she had her children go out and kill a chicken, prepare it and she ate it alone in her room! It's interesting that only two or three of her children ever married. Nancy Siler died on January 18, 1943. In 1984 there were only fifteen descendants.

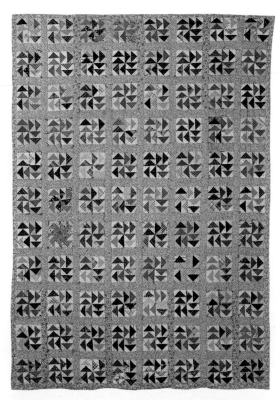

Dutchman's Puzzle, made by Edith Dearfield, c. 1920, Corvallis, Oregon, 66" x 93 1/2". (Collection of Carol Harker, Bothell, Washington)

Applique Quilts

Applique quilts remained popular during these years, particularly in the more affluent East and South. But, because they usually required new cloth to execute their careful color schemes, applique quilts often lacked the earthy exuberance of the scrap bag quilts from the same era.

---

33. *Irwin, A PEOPLE AND THEIR QUILTS, p. 93.*

Most women could not afford to purchase the large amounts of new fabric needed for these quilts. In addition, their domestic routines were far too busy and the need for bedcovers too strong to allow them to make an applique quilt.

Floral designs were also a popular theme, as can be seen in the many red and green quilts created in the mid-19th century. However, the popularity of red and green quilts faded in the last quarter of the 19th century.

Double Peony, Edwards family quilt, c. 1825, Kentucky, 90'' x 108''. This glorious quilt recently emerged stained and discolored from a trunk where it had been for more than a century. (Collection of George and Maurene Edwards, Seattle, Washington)

Detail: Applique Album Quilt Inscription
To Mrs. J. Walton
> Should sorrow o'er thy brow,
> It's darkened shadow fling
> And hopes that cheer thee now
> Die in their early spring
>
> If like the weary dove
> Or shoreless ocean driven
> Raise thou thine eyes above
> There's rest for thee in heaven
>
> Still let not every thought
> To this poor world be given
> Nor always be forgot
> Thy better rest in heaven.
> > A Friend
> > Canal Dover
> > June 12, 1849

Detail: Applique Album Quilt Inscription
> Tis sweet to know that one pure heart
> Forever thinks with mine
> Nor with this knowledge soon impart
> Nor this pure heart resign.
> > Canal Dover
> > June 10
> > Ann McMichael

Quilters As Historians

While men recorded the events of the age or their lives in paintings, women kept a record of their lives and the lives of their families in stitches. Men were the portrait painters, silhouette makers, and artists, while women were merely indulging in domestic needlework.

Album Quilts

Album quilts were one way quilters commemorated events in their lives. An album quilt features a variety of blocks, often consisting of applique patterns. Many album quilts have the name of the maker inscribed or embroidered on them.

While some Album Quilts were made by individuals, others were made by groups. Frequently the latter were "Presentation Quilts," testimonials to a minister or his wife, or a valued teacher or other public figure. There were "Friendship Quilts" made for a departing friend or as a token of affection and remembrance when an engagement was announced. A variation was the "Friendship Medley Quilt" in which friends made and signed blocks which were made of the same pattern but to which they had contributed different fabrics.[34]

The heyday of the friendship quilt was from 1840—1875. At that time steel pen points and improved inks made writing on cloth easier and more permanent. Many different patterns were used in friendship quilts, but Chimney Sweep and Album Patch were the favorites.

34. Sienkiewicz, SPOKEN WITHOUT A WORD, p. 17.

Applique Album Quilt, made by Lizetta Hicksecker, c. 1849, Canal Dover, Ohio, 71'' x 79''. Appliqued squares with poetry inscriptions. (Collection of Museum of History and Industry, Seattle, Washington)

Bridal Quilts

The finest and most intricate quilt made to commemorate a special event was the bridal quilt. Although sometimes made by a member of the family or a group of friends, the bridal quilt was usually made to showcase the bride's most skillful needlework.

The Bridal Quilt was begun after the young woman's engagement had been announced. By the time she was engaged a woman had customarily completed twelve quilt tops which were then quilted up before her marriage, as the expense of padding and backing would only be undertaken when a new household was in preparation.

...Bridal Quilts were used after the wedding only on special occasions, or for honored guests, and have frequently come down to us without ever having been laundered. They were virtually always applique, and it was customary to incorporate hearts either into the applique or in the quilting. But it was considered bad luck for a woman to use hearts in a quilt before her engagement had been announced.[35]

Double Wedding Ring Quilt, made by Emma Mittendorf and Eva Fogle, 1930s, York, Pennsylvania, 74 1/2" x 83 1/2". Made as a wedding gift for Jack and Sylvia Mittendorf by his grandmother and great-grandmother. (Collection of Sylvia and Jack Mittendorf, Seattle, Washington)

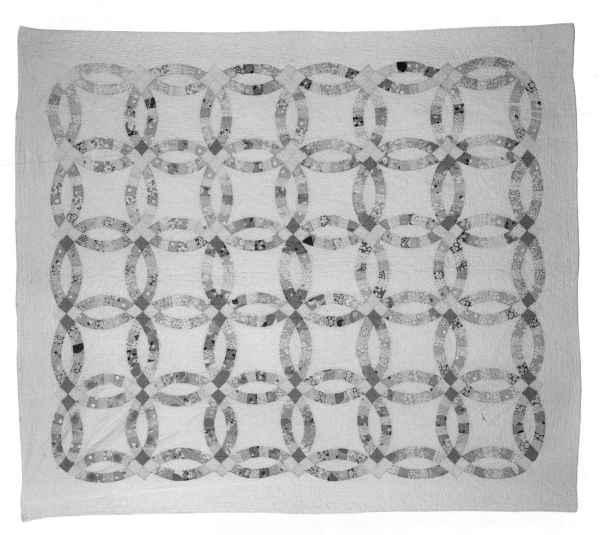

35. Mainardi, QUILTS, THE GREAT AMERICAN ART, p. 27.

The Rose Quilt bearing the names of Martin J. Carothers and Elizabeth E. Carothers, 16 March 1849, appears to be a bridal quilt made by a group of friends. Martin J. Carothers was a Methodist minister at Mt. Rock in Cumberland County, Pennsylvania. The blocks indicate several persons worked on the quilt, covering it with elaborate quilting motifs, including a tree (tree of life?), a hand, oak leaves, and several pairs of scissors, as well as detailed inscriptions done in fine quilting stitches: "1849," "March the 21," "Cumberland County." The rose is red; the rest is green.

President's Wreath, maker unknown, 1849, Mt. Rock, Pennsylvania, 95" x 95". Made as a presentation quilt for the marriage of Reverend Martin J. Carothers and Elizabeth E. Carothers. (Collection of That Patchwork Place, Inc., Bothell, Washington)

Detail: Inscription on Reverend Martin J. Carothers presentation quilt. Note scissors quilted in upper corner of block.

Throughout quiltmaking history the Bride's Quilt was particularly important to American women. Its making was a rite whose precepts gave a tangible outlet to all the yearnings of a young woman for love and marriage, and to the heartfelt hopes of her friends and relatives that it be a fruitful match; one in which the couple's joys would outweigh their sorrows.

Even before the Victorian Period's passion for expressing religious, moral, and romantic sentiments explicitly in writing and implicitly through symbols, that most womanly Album Quilt of all, the "Bride's Quilt," had its own constellation of symbols: the rose, the heart, lovebirds and doves*, linked rings.

Bridal Quilt customs and styles varied. Elegant white on white quilts were the vogue for three quarters of a century until 1850, while the Double Wedding Ring pattern, popular since the late 1800s, remains a favorite today. The "Rose of Sharon" applique pattern was a Bridal Quilt favorite of long duration and led the way for the "Applique Album Bridal Quilts."[36]

Women continue to use the bridal quilt motifs (hearts, doves, flowers) when they design quilts to commemorate special days in their lives such as anniversaries.

Hearts and Flowers, made by Marjorie L. Meyers, 1985, Bothell, Washington, 84" x 104". Quilt adapted to include 30 hearts for a gift to her husband in commemoration of their 30th anniversary. (Collection of the artist)

36. Sienkiewicz, SPOKEN WITHOUT A WORD, p. 17.

*Doves were chosen as a symbol for loyalty. Doves mate for life and do not take on another mate after the death of their only mate.

Baby Quilts

In 19th-century America, women's duties were well defined: to attend to the household and to bear large numbers of children.

> Only by continual childbearing could the 18th- and 19th-century woman fulfill her life's obligations: her obligation to God, as set down in the Scriptures, that she should be fruitful and multiply; her obligation to her husband and family as each child represented an additional economic unit; and her obligation to her country, a pioneer society intent on expanding the population and the frontiers of a developing nation.
>
> ...The rate of infant mortality was staggering. Women married young, bore children at regular and frequent intervals, and all too often died before middle age.[37]

Since children were viewed as miniature adults, most of the baby quilts made during this period, were adult quilts made small. The elements were identical to those used in adult quilts—color, design, and fabrics—except they were reduced in scale so that they could be used by children.

The birth of a child was a joyous occasion in poor households, where there was seldom reason to rejoice. Indeed, the birth of the first child was celebrated, especially if the wife had borne a son. The wedding night was considered a success only if a child was produced nine months later.

> "Martin Carothers and Ellen Duffy were married October 12, 1827. An infant would have been conceived in June or July of 1828 which might be a little late for a first pregnancy in those days."[38]

The quilts made by thrifty women of meager households were truly treasured. Nancyann Twelker tells of the baby quilt that has been handed down in her family:

> My baby quilt, made by my great grandmother, Nancy Tucker McCurdy, in 1933 was used not only by me, but by my brother and sister and then all of our children. My great grandmother had only one pair of good shoes made of high-top black leather. As these shoes wore out she relegated them to lesser purposes—everyday shoes, gardening shoes. Finally she would cut off the leather from the top and sew it around her finger as protection for the hand that was under the quilt.

LeMoyne Star, origin unknown, c. 1850, 36" x 48". Interesting old calico prints are found in this pieced quilt said to have crossed the plains in 1852. It features a Dogtooth border and clam shell quilting pattern. (Collection of Museum of History and Industry, Seattle, Washington)

37. *Sandi Fox, SMALL ENDEARMENTS, p. 2.*

38. *Cumberland Associates, Carlisle, Pa., to Nancy J. Martin, 19 February 1986.*

Freedom Quilts

Freedom quilts were a popular way to celebrate a young man's independence. This custom has continued through the years, with present day freedom quilts being made for both males and females.

> The Freedom Quilt was made for a young man on his 21st birthday by all his female friends at a party arranged by his mother and sisters—a custom popular until approximately 1825. The significance of the 21st birthday was that a young man was legally free at that age whereas previously his labor and wages legally belonged to his father. There was no Freedom Quilt for women, since their labor legally belonged to their father until marriage and afterwards to their husband.[39]

> "Freedom quilts might be full of metamorphic designs and moral inscriptions. Mother's 'last say' as it were. Presented to the young man when he became of age at 21, the quilt could then be put away to become his gift to his bride when he married."[40]

Mourning Quilts

Many early examples of American folk art have death or mourning as their subject matter. Much death-related art in textiles was created during this period, such as painted and embroidered mourning and memorial pictures and elaborate tombstones. The weeping willow tree, a sign of mourning, is often found as an expression of grief.

Mourning quilts were often made to commemorate the death of a family member. The most famous of these quilts is the Graveyard Quilt, made by Elizabeth Roseberry Mitchell in 1839. Coffins bearing family names were to be moved from the edges of the quilt to the center burial plot upon the death of a family member.

Another type of mourning quilt was the "Death Watch Quilt." While sitting by the bed of a dying relative, each person made a quilt block, sometimes using fabric from the dying person's clothing.[41]

39. Mainardi, QUILTS, THE GREAT AMERICAN ART, p. 27.

40. Sienkiewicz, SPOKEN WITHOUT A WORD, p. 17.

41. Ibid.

Hexagon Mosaic, origin unknown, c. 1890, 73" x 82". (Collection of Toni Flink, Seattle, Washington)

Pineapple, maker unknown, c. 1900, Portland, Oregon, 73" x 88". (Collection of Nancyann Johanson Twelker, Edmonds, Washington)

Silk Diamonds, origin unknown, c. 1900, Portland, Oregon, 78" x 92". (Collection of Joanne Starr, Clinton, Washington)

Victorian Quilts 1870—1900

The "crazy quilt," which was not really a quilt at all, emerged during the Victorian era. Usually made as couch throws or slumber robes, these quilts were so delicate and fragile that they were rarely used.

As America became more industrialized and technology brought many improvements to the home, the role of the woman of the household changed. In striving to be "middle class," the man wanted his wife viewed as a "lady." She was a visual extension of his success and it was important that she no longer be associated with domestic chores and crafts that were "make do." The "lady" was to spend her leisure hours doing delicate needlework and fancy embroidery on the most opulent fabrics, which she would use to decorate her ornate Victorian parlor. Thus, patchwork and the making of useful bed quilts fell out of favor.

Log Cabin, made by mother of Helene Nebel Willsey, c. 1850, Onconta, New York, 53" x 54". Excellent use of plaid silks and taffetas set in a "barnraising" design. (Collection of Patricia R. Dunning, Marysville, Washington)

Pieced from the best silks, satins and velvets (materials newly available to the growing middle class), the patchwork throws of this era are rich mosaics of color and texture. Fine quilting was no longer the skill of importance; proficiency in embroidery and the mastering of a multitude of stitch types was emphasized. The women's magazines of the day, promoting an opulence of dress and home decoration made possible by the advances of industry, helped to perpetuate this new quilting style by printing detailed embroidery instructions.

In an unprecedented outpouring of sentimentality, Victorian quilters filled their work with bits and pieces of their personal past: Father's vest pocket, lace from a wedding veil, ribbons commemorating political events or visits to faraway lands. A penchant for romantic themes is also evident, as is a love of oriental motifs. This latter obsession was probably inspired by America's exposure to the glories of Japanese culture during the Philadelphia Centennial exhibition of 1876.[42]

Autograph albums, in which poems, verses, and signatures were inscribed, became very popular during the Victorian era. Thus, many of the crazy quilts made during this time contained inscriptions, Biblical verses, and signatures. Family autograph quilts were made by a single quiltmaker or family groups and then signed by family members.

The evolution of American quiltmaking had come to a halt. Early quilts, although not at all decorative, were useful for keeping warm. Then the patchwork quilt, a work of art in addition to being a functional bed covering, evolved. And finally came the crazy quilt, beautiful to behold with little, if any, utilitarian purpose.

Spider Web quilt top, made by Joseph Spark, c. 1890, New York, 60" x 77". Made by a tailor who had access to a marvelous collection of silks. (Collection of Museum of History and Industry, Seattle, Washington)

42.   Smith, "A Legacy of Quilts," p. 69.

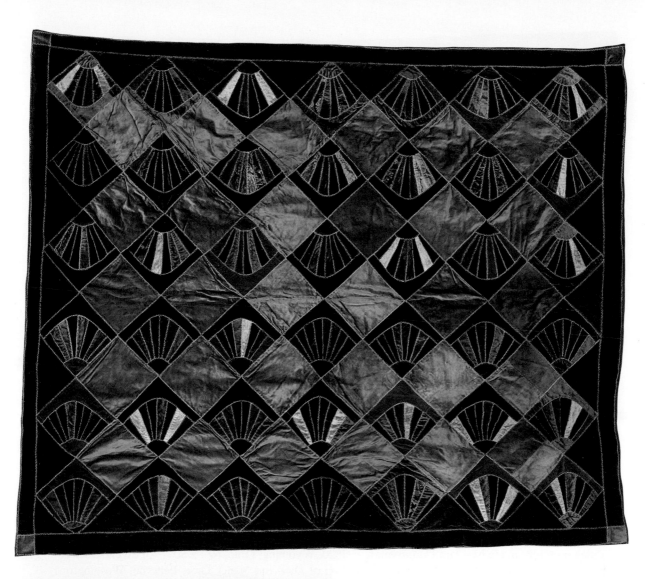

Grandmother's Fan, made by Mrs. D. M. Walters, c. 1908, 71" x 83". Worked in plush velveteen fabrics, this quilt won a medal at the Alaska Yukon Exposition in 1909. (Collection of Museum of History and Industry, Seattle, Washington)

Cigar Band Quilt, origin unknown, c. 1890, 63" x 77". A Victorian quilt pieced from the silk ribbons which held cigars in their boxes. (Collection of Museum of History and Industry, Seattle, Washington)

Four Patch quilt top, made by Clara Countryman, c. 1920, Wyoming, Ohio, 69" x 80". An excellent selection of dark print fabrics are set "barnraising" style. (Collection of Dick and Nancy Dice, Bellevue, Washington)

Triangles, maker unknown, c. 1900, Pennsylvania 69 1/2" x 72". The clam shell design was used to quilt the red triangles. (Collection of That Patchwork Place, Inc., Bothell, Washington)

43. Barbara Brackman, "Dating Old Quilts, Part Three: Cotton Prints 1890—1960," QUILTER'S NEWSLETTER MAGAZINE, Nov. 1984, p. 16.

Dark Print Quilts 1890—1925

Around the turn of the century, quilts made with dark red, pink, navy blue, a light gray blue, black, and gray prints were a fad. Fabrics during this period were printed with small-scale florals, sprigs, and geometrics in one color on a white background. Inexpensive to produce, these fabrics were of lesser quality and contained less detail than the earlier prints. Dots and lines for shading were used sparingly.

Also found in quilts made in this time period were the black and white prints that appeared gray. These somber prints were referred to as "Shaker Grays" or "Mourning Prints." but the quilter created exuberant color schemes from these fabrics by combining them with the brighter dark reds and pinks.

These small, dark calicoes were popular for the home-sewn clothing, "children's waists and ladies' wrappers," so it is not unusual that the scraps appeared in the quilts produced during this period.[43]

Philadelphia Pavements, made by Ruth Moritz, c. 1920, Wisconsin, 80" x 92". (Collection of Jack and Sylvia Mittendorf, Seattle, Washington)

Grandmother's Fan, origin unknown, c. 1930, 81" x 93". (Collection of Shirley Thompson, Edmonds, Washington)

Double Irish Chain, origin unknown, c. 1910, 82" x 82". (Collection of That Patchwork Place, Inc., Bothell, Washington)

Grandmother's Flower Garden, origin unknown, c. 1920, 58 1/2" x 79 1/2". (Collection of Sue Saltkill, Woodinville, Washington)

Double Wedding Ring, made by Emma Mittendorf and Eva Fogle, 1930s, York, Pennsylvania, 74 1/2" x 83 1/2". (Collection of Jack and Sylvia Mittendorf, Seattle, Washington)

Dresden Plate, made by Wilhemenia Ruffing, 1915, Whitehall, Pennsylvania, 80" x 80". (Collection of That Patchwork Place, Inc., Bothell, Washington)

Quilt Revival

In 1910 a period where quilts were given widespread publicity emerged. Many organizations not normally associated with quilts took an interest, thus producing many new quilters.

While there have always been a large number of women who engage in quiltmaking, the decline in popularity of the Victorian crazy quilt in 1900 resulted in less general interest and publicity. The farm women, who represented a large portion of America's quilters, had rejected the fragile silk crazy quilt as inappropriate to their homes. They preferred quilts to the machine-made bed coverings available at the time. "I think quilts made from Calico scraps are cheaper than the 'soft, fleecy blankets' for those who economize."[44]

Collecting antiques became all the rage, and the art of quilting experienced an unprecedented renaissance. The typical quilts born of this nostalgia were not children of necessity; warm, woolen blankets were readily available at the nearest department store. Instead, many women bought yardage specifically for their quilted creations, indulging in the rainbow of pastel hues—watermelon-pinks, mint-greens, and lemon-yellows—that saturated the market.[45]

44. Cuesta Benberry, "The 20th Century's First Quilt Revival," *QUILTER'S NEWSLETTER MAGAZINE,* July/Aug. 1979, p. 20.

45. Smith, "A Legacy of Quilts," p. 71.

Many factors contributed to the quilt revival of 1910. Among them was a reaction against Victorian home decor and architecture. Both men and women were rejecting the "gingerbread" trim on the outside and the overdecorated parlors on the inside.

In the early 1900s there was a return to classic architecture with clean-cut lines and simple unpretentious furnishings. Colonial homes, Cape Cod cottages, and the bungalow, with appropriate furnishings, became popular. This, in turn, caused an increased interest in patchwork quilts, which blended perfectly with the colonial and Cape Cod decor.

Women began to search for old patchwork quilts for their homes or decided to make their own. In "Revival of Patchwork," the editors of *Modern Priscilla* noted, "Every woman who is fortunated enough to possess one of the patchwork quilts of the ante-bellum period is displaying it proudly as part of her guest bedroom equipment."[46]

World War I, which erupted in Europe in 1914, also affected the quilt revival. Many relief committees, such as the Serbian Distress Fund, the Polish Relief Association, and the Belgian Relief Fund, actively sought the inclusion of patchwork quilts in packages sent to war-torn Europe.

Many organizations embarked on fund-raising activities to support the Red Cross. In December, 1917, *Modern Priscilla* featured an article "One Thousand Dollars for the Red Cross Can Be Raised On A Memorial Quilt." The article explained fully the procedures necessary to accomplish this goal, the prices to charge for the squares according to their placement on the quilt top, and it (The organization charged a small sum to embroider names on the quilt, which was then raffled off or auctioned. All monies raised were donated to the Red Cross.) also showed a model of the ticket form for selling signature blanks. Full pattern instructions were given as to construction, color, and yardages.[47]

However, it is after the United States' entry into World War I in 1917 that we can see a direct relationship between the war and quilts. The U.S. government then actively urged its citizens to make quilts using this slogan in numerous newspaper and magazine ads: "MAKE QUILTS—SAVE THE BLANKETS FOR OUR BOYS OVER THERE."

Since the government had taken the entire "wool clip for the coming year," factories would not be able to make blankets for the civilian population.

Adopting the slogan, *Modern Priscilla* magazine featured an article in the September 1918 issue, "Calling the Quilts Into Service For Our Country." Four quilt patterns were offered; one was a design to be quilted on the sewing machine. Numerous utilitarian quilts for home front use were made in response to the slogan. These quilts, regardless of their actual patterns soon earned the nickname "Liberty Quilts."[48]

Red Cross Quilt, origin unknown, c. 1917, 72" x 72". Signatures were penned onto the squares of this raffle quilt made to raise money for the Red Cross. (Collection of Carol Walkky, Seattle, Washington)

46. Benberry, "The 20th Century's First Quilt Revival," Sept. 1979, p. 25.

47. Benberry, "The 20th Century's First Quilt Revival," Oct. 1979, p. 10.

48. Ibid.

49. Ruby McKim, 101 PATCHWORK PATTERNS, 1962.

It was the newspapers who helped spread the growth of quilting with their regular quilting columns. The most famous of these were the *Kansas City Star* columns and the patterns from the McKim Studio by Ruby McKim.[49]

Some very competent writer-researchers engaged in the most thorough investigations of American quilts ever attempted until that time. They brought to public view rare and extraordinary old quilts which displayed dimensions of creativity in the American quiltmaker most people never knew existed. In addition, these writer-researchers enriched quilt lore. They got into print much that had been preserved only by oral tradition in very restricted locales.

All of this proved fascinating to the public, and served as a stimulus to deeper involvement in old quilts and new quiltmaking. "No form of needlework is in greater vogue at the present time than patchwork," states a 1916 source.[50]

Smaller newspapers or those in more remote areas soon followed suit. Quilt contests and quilt exhibits were prevalent as a result of the newspaper columns. The *Seattle Post Intelligencer* published a pamphlet in 1927 featuring photos and patterns for several of the contest quilts.

Avid quilters collected these columns, often pasting them in notebooks or composition books. Many quilt patterns were ordered by mail from these newspaper columns.

Another trend which gained momentum was apparent in the national periodicals such as *Delineator, Ladies Home Journal, Harper's Bazaar, House Beautiful, Woman's Home Companion, Pictorial Review, Country Life* and *Modern Priscilla.* It was a nostalgic, "looking-back" at the quilts their grandmothers had made as examples of imagination, thrift, industriousness and skill. In the early 1900s issues, complete admiration and full acceptance of the old quilts were not yet forthcoming. Admiration, yes, but tempered by such terms as "odd," "queer," "crude," or "quaint."[51]

From the influential women's periodical, *Ladies Home Journal,* emerged some of the most distinguished writer-researchers of the period. They were Mrs. Leopold Simon, Elizabeth Daingerfield, and Marie D. Webster.

Marie D. Webster's quilt designs appeared in *Ladies Home Journal* and *Ladies Home Journal Embroidery Book* from 1911 to 1915. The majority of the designs were her originals, and a few were her adaptations of old patterns. Her designing talent was so prodigious that today we can say without a fear of contradiction that Marie Webster has been the single "most copied" quilt designer in the 20th century. Not only did she produce her soon to be legendary designs at the time of the revival, but she

Churn Dash, origin unknown, c. 1900, 70" x 90". A true scrap quilt given exuberance by the use of striped fabrics. The Baptist Fan quilting pattern unifies the quilt top. (Collection of That Patchwork Place, Inc., Bothell, Washington)

Detail: Elizabeth Dearfield's quilting notebooks and patterns.

---

50. Benberry, "The 20th Century's First Quilt Revival," Sept. 1979, p. 25.

51. Benberry, "The 20th Century's First Quilt Revival," July/Aug. 1979, p. 21.

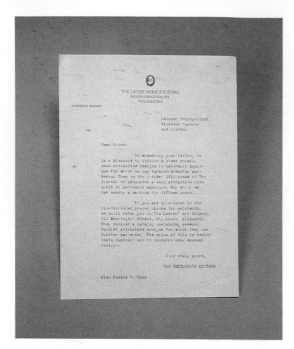

Detail: Letter dated 1916 from *Ladies Home Journal.*

authored the first full-length quilt book ever written in the United States. Her *Quilts: Their Story and How To Make Them,* published in 1915, was a milestone in the first quilt revival.[52]

Although *Godey's Lady's Book* from an earlier era is generally credited as an influence on quilting, Jonathan Holstein presents information leading one to believe otherwise.

> It has often been said that many of them (quilt patterns) came from ladies' magazines of the nineteenth century, particularly *Godey's Lady's Book,* a magazine for the middle class and those aspiring to it. But a reading of its entire run from its inception in 1830 to its last issue in 1898 revealed only some seventy-five patterns for pieced work; of these, fewer than five were designed in block-style, the rest were to be made of small components each pieced to the next in the ancient manner...
> *Godey's,* it seems, was catering more to the later nineteenth century craze for silk pieced work, performed as a genteel pastime, than to those who made quilts of cotton and wool to keep their families warm.[53]

As mentioned earlier, farm women were the mainstay of quiltmakers. Quilting columns appeared in the rural magazines of the 1920s and 1930s, such as *Farm and Fireside, Rural Progress, Ohio Farmer, Orange Judd Farmer, National Stockman and Farmer,* and *Hearth and Home.* These magazines were avidly subscribed to by farmers and their wives who lived in the more remote areas.

In addition to the farm papers, quiltmakers had two other excellent sources of quilt patterns available to them. One was *Diagrams of Quilt, Sofa and Pin Cushion Patterns,* from the Ladies Art Company Catalog. It had been published since the late 1800s and offered 420 traditional quilt patterns.

> I think the publication of the Ladies Art Catalog in the late 1800s was sort of earthshaking. It was the first time one publication offered to the public, a catalog with at least 300 patterns at a reasonable price with names assigned to them. The majority were pieced. They were not original patterns, but rather patterns in use at that time compiled or gathered from other periodicals and almanacs.
> The company claimed that by the 1920s, their mail order business employed 50 people. They didn't sell just quilt patterns, but that was their main offering. There were undoubtedly other companies who may have sold patterns into a limited area, but Ladies Art from the beginning must have intended to go national, since they ran ads for their catalog in the *Good Housekeeping Magazine.*[54]

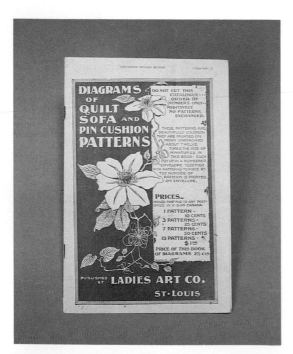

Detail: Ladies Art Catalog

52. Benberry, "The 20th Century's First Quilt Revival," Sept. 1979, p. 25—26

53. Holstein, THE PIECED QUILT, AN AMERICAN DESIGN TRADITION, p. 56.

54. Joyce Gross, "Cuesta Benberry: Part II Significant Milestones for Quilters," QUILTERS JOURNAL, No. 24, March 1984, p. 24.

Later, about 1910, the *Catalog Practical Needlework—Quilt Patterns,* by Clara A. Stone, offered 186 traditional quilt patterns. This catalog appears to be an outgrowth of her contributions to *Hearth and Home* and has a New England—East Coast orientation to its name.[55]

Mail order kits for quilts were also available from magazine and catalog sources.

The early 1900s was a time of tremendous population shifts, and the United States became an urban society, rather than a rural one. Although not all persons who used these stamped cloth kits were urban dwellers, it is likely that a great many were.[56]

Done in pastel colors of the 1920s, these pieced and appliqued masterpieces still carry the blue stampings that were used to guide the placement of the quilting design.

Pineapple quilt top, made by Celia Mortensen, c. 1940, Modesto, California, 82" x 104". (Collection of Joanne Starr, Clinton, Washington)

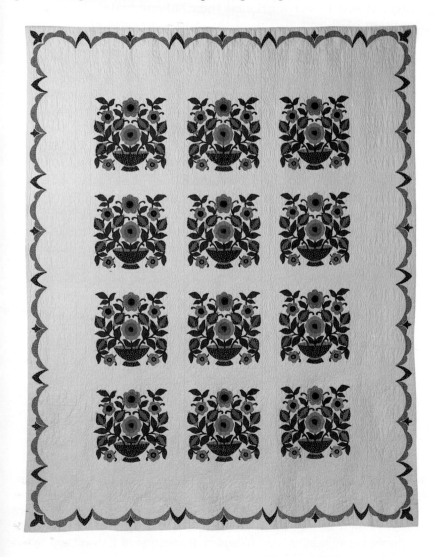

Urn of Flowers, origin unknown, c. 1920, 76" x 97". Beautiful example of a quilt made from a mail order kit. Blue dots from the quilt pattern stamping still remain. (Collection of That Patchwork Place, Inc., Bothell, Washington)

55. Benberry, "The 20th Century's First Quilt Revival," July/Aug. 1979, p. 21.

56. Ibid.

Detail: Early batting wrappers from Stearns and Foster's Mountain Mist batting and the Rock River Cotton Company's Crown Jewel batting.

Batting companies, who benefited from this resurgence of quilting in the 1920s and 1930s, also helped the quilting revival by sponsoring contests and printing patterns on the inside of the batting wrapper. One company, the Rock River Cotton Company, offered a full-sized roll of their Crown Batting free to anyone sending in ten Crown Jewel trademarks cut from wrappers.

The Stearns and Foster Company, a batting producer dating back to 1846, has sponsored many projects to promote quilting and preserve its history. They began printing patterns on the inside of their batting wrappers in 1929. In the 1920s and 1930s serious quilters nationwide were commissioned to develop new patterns based on traditional favorites. These quilts were exhibited in store windows and displays to promote and advertise quiltmaking. Then in 1949, Stearns and Foster sponsored the Central States Quilt Exhibition, which consisted of prize-winning quilts from state fairs. The patterns were printed inside the Stearns and Foster wrappers.

Stearns and Foster marketed their batting under the name of Mountain Mist and also used this name on catalogs.

Mountain Mist published their first catalog in 1931. The publication of the patterns had a great influence in the selection of patterns used on quilts in the 20th century, e.g., "NY Beauty" has just assumed the name that Mountain Mist gave it in the 1930s. Previously the pattern was known as "Crown of Thorns" or "Rocky Mountain Rose," but today it is almost universally called "NY Beauty"—even a lot of learned journals use that name. In fact, one seldom hears the original name, and I think it is due to the influence of those Mountain Mist patterns.[57]

Basket of Flowers, made by Mary McLaughlin, c. 1940, Bellingham, Washington, 82" x 93". Mary McLaughlin made quilts for all the children and grandchildren in her family. The pieced and appliqued baskets were started in 1938 from a kit which included stamped designs for the quilting. It was finished in 1986 by Sylvia McFadden. (Collection of Edward and Sylvia McFadden, Stanwood, Washington)

57. Gross, "Cuesta Benberry: Part II Significant Milestones for Quilters," p. 24.

Several popular patterns emerged during this period, among them, Sunbonnet Sue, Double Wedding Ring, and the Dresden Plate. Sunbonnet Sue had first appeared with her partner Overall Bill as outline embroidery in the late 1880s. Betty Hagerman, in *A Meeting of the Sunbonnet Children,* indicates that these patterns for applique appeared around 1910. Kate Greenaway, who was a popular English illustrator of children's books and whose drawings exerted a tremendous influence on children's fashions, is sometimes thought to be the originator of the Sunbonnet children. However, Bertha Corbett, an American artist who was acquainted with Kate Greenaway's illustrations, is actually responsible for "igniting the Sunbonnet spark in the United States."[58]

Sunbonnet Sue, origin unknown, c. 1930, Pennsylvania, 45" x 60". Old blocks using feedsack prints were quilted in 1981 by Freda Smith. (Collection of That Patchwork Place, Inc., Bothell, Washington)

Sunbonnet Sue, made by Lillian Burch, c. 1932, Colorado, 63" x 74". In 1974, the maker set together old blocks she and her mother made in 1932 from childhood dresses. A teacup quilting design is used in the lattice strips. (Collection of the artist)

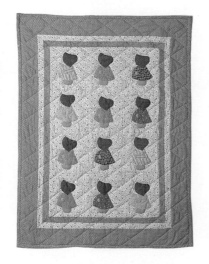 

Sunbonnet Sue, made by Nancy Martin, 1985, Woodinville, Washington, 27" x 36" for the birth of Sara Jane Martin.

Overall Bill, made by Nancy Martin, 1985, Woodinville, Washington, 27" x 36" for the birth of Steven David Martin.

---

58. Betty J. Hagerman, *A MEETING OF THE SUNBONNET CHILDREN, p. 7.*

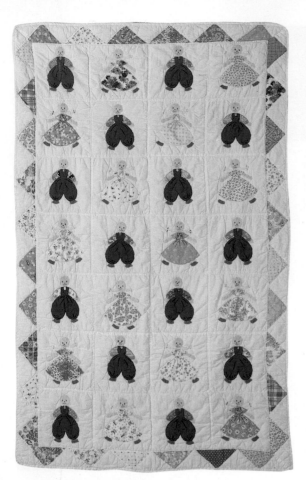

Raggedy Ann & Raggedy Andy, made by Eldra Pebsworth, 1960, Seattle, Washington, 38" x 56". Made from an Aunt Martha's pattern for the birth of her grandson Paul Bartow.

It was during this period that quilts with juvenile themes for the nursery and young children emerged. In the early 19th century embroidered picture quilts done in turkey red on a white background were very popular. The pieces were of interest to children, and several featured Sunbonnet children. Many of the stamped designs could be ordered from the Ladies Art Company Catalog, *Diagrams of Quilt, Sofa, and Pin Cushion Patterns.* Numerous alphabet blocks, including pieced and stamped designs, also appeared in this catalog.

General needlework sources, such as Valley Supply Company, St. Louis, Missouri, offered "kindergarten blocks." These were 9-inch outline embroidered blocks, often with a pictorial theme taken from nursery rhymes or folk tales. Most were to be embroidered in turkey red, and were to make crib quilts, or to teach young children to sew.[59]

Ruby Short McKim designed an outline embroidery quilt, the Colonial History quilt, which was widely distributed in the 1930s. Many children learned their American history from this popular pattern.

Other juvenile themes appeared during this period including many in commercial kits. Themes ranged from storybook characters (Raggedy Ann and Andy, the Three Bears) to toy soldiers, dolls and marionette shows.

All of these designs marked the realization that the child was indeed a unique, distinct personality with distinct interests, not a miniature adult. No longer were crib quilts miniaturized versions of adult patterns.

Colonial History Quilt, origin unknown, c. 1930, 66" x 95". (Collection of Bonnie Leman, Wheatridge, Colorado)

59. Benberry, "The 20th Century's First Quilt Revival," Sept. 1979, p. 29.

Judging from the number of samples that have survived, the Double Wedding Ring was an extremely popular pattern. According to quilt historian Barbara Brackman:

> The Double Wedding Ring has 19th-century roots, probably based on the Pickle Dish pattern. "Double Wedding Ring" quilts made before the epidemic of the thirties are rare. I have been able to find only one example from before World War I. The Baltimore Museum of Art owns one donated by Dr. William Rush Dunton, a quilt historian of the 1940s. He dated the quilt as from around 1870.[60]

The Dresden Plate is another distinctive 20th century pattern. It is undoubtedly an old, rather uncommon design that enjoyed an amazing burst of popularity in the second quarter of this century.

> The oldest dated quilt made in the United States (Ann Tuel's Marriage Quilt, 1785) has a Dresden plate in the center. The earlier designs have a circular edge; the variations with the scalloped edges seem to date from the last quarter of the 19th century when fan quilts were popular. The oldest reference to the name Dresden Plate is in Ruby McKim's *101 Patchwork Patterns* from the late 1920s. She calls the design Dresden Plate, Friendship Ring and a Star.
>
> The inspiration for the name Dresden Plate seems obvious. The pattern does bear resemblance to a china plate and Dresden china from factories in Dresden, Germany and was highly prized in the 19th and early 20th century.[61]

The popularity of the fan quilt pattern, which originated during the Victorian crazy quilt period, emerged again in the 1920s, when the fan spokes were made from scraps of pastel prints.

Three Bears Quilt, origin unknown, c. 1920, 32" x 53". (Collection of Diane Coombs, Everett, Washington)

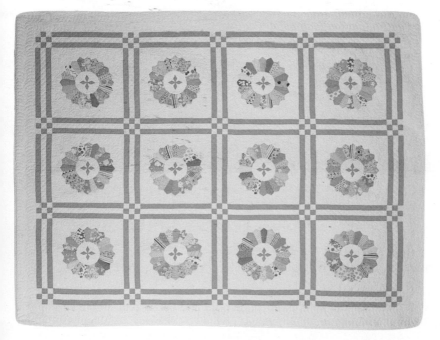

Dresden Plate, pieced in 1930s by unknown maker, finished in 1978 by Donna Hanson Eines, Edmonds, Washington, 88" x 110". (Collection of the artist)

---

60. Brackman, "Patterns to Ponder," QUILT WORLD OMNIBOOK, Winter 1983, p. 13.

61. Brackman, "Patterns to Ponder," QUILT WORLD OMNIBOOK, Fall 1985, p. 6.

Feedsack Quilts 1925—1940

Many people call the quilts from between the World Wars "feedsack quilts," recalling that sacks for grain and seed were made of the same cotton prints as the quilts, and that indeed many of the quilts were actually made from the recycled sacks. The feedsack cottons and the medium-weight dress prints that we see used in the Depression era were inexpensive, but unlike the cheap, dark prints of the turn of the century, they were multi-colored. By the mid-1920s technology had advanced to the point where a piece of cloth could be printed several times in different colors but still was cheap enough to use for a feed sack.[62]

Using actual feedsack materials often resulted in erratic designs. Nancyann Twelker explains the quilt made by her mother, Lulu McCurdy Johanson:

Mother's quilt was made from the leftover parts of the feedsacks after my great aunt had used the best parts for her quilt. Mother had to arrange the flowers and wreaths so that they covered up the holes that the strings from the feedsack had made.

Rose Wreath Quilt, made by Lulu McCurdy Johanson, 1927, Tacoma, Washington, 38 1/2" x 50". Made by a sixteen-year-old girl from scraps of flour sacks. (Collection of Nancyann Johanson Twelker, Seattle, Washington)

Double Wedding Ring, origin unknown, c. 1930, 67" x 84". (Collection of Donna Hanson Eines, Edmonds, Washington)

Grandmother's Flower Garden, origin unknown, c. 1930, 70" x 86". (Collection of Jack and Sylvia Mittendorf, Seattle, Washington)

Sunbonnet Sue, origin unknown, c. 1930, Pennsylvania, 45" x 60". (Collection of That Patchwork Place, Inc., Bothell, Washington)

Cherry Basket, origin unknown, c. 1930, 71" x 84". Flour sacks were used for the print and background fabrics of this quilt. (Collection of Marsha McCloskey, Seattle, Washington)

Women reveled in the quantity of prints available at this time and continued to make "scrap type" quilts using a profusion of the available pastel prints. Packets of scraps could now be ordered for a reasonable price, from mail-order companies who advertised in ladies' magazines.

Interest in quilts and quiltmaking, which had reached "revival" proportions in the 1930s, declined.

Fewer publications carried quilts in the 1940s and 1950s, although there were some important quilt figures and some very important quilts being made. Florence Peto, Bertha Stenge, Rose Kretsinger, Charlotte Jane Whitehill and many others kept the quilt tradition alive and built on our heritage. But for Americans as a whole, there was little to observe.[63]

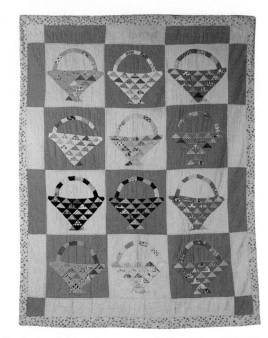

Basket, origin unknown, c. 1930, 62" x 79". (Collection of Rosalie Pfeifer, Kent, Washington)

Hexagon Stars, made by Lenora Gregg Marsh, c. 1930, Hastings, Nebraska, 70" x 82". Made from two different scrap collections, this exuberant quilt displays wonderful fabric combinations. (Collection of Marsha McCloskey, Seattle, Washington)

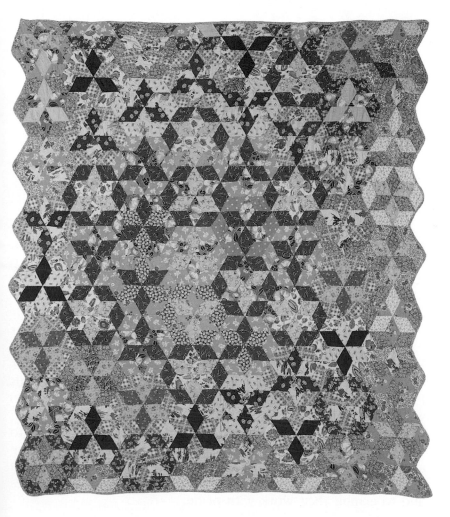

62. Brackman, "Dating Old Quilts, Part Three: Cotton Prints 1890—1960," p. 16.

63. Gross, "Cuesta Benberry: Part II Significant Milestones for Quilters," p. 24.

Homespun Houses, made by Nancy Martin, 1985, Woodinville, Washington, 72" x 96". Scraps of homespun are used for houses set in a "barnraising" design. Hanging Diamonds, a traditional quilting design, was quilted by Andrea Scadden. (Collection of That Patchwork Place, Inc., Bothell, Washington)

Underground Railway, made by Marsha Mc-Closkey, Seattle, Washington, 1982, 42" x 54". (Collection of That Patchwork Place, Inc., Bothell, Washington)

Quilt Awakening

A "back to the earth" movement began to take shape in the 1960s as a reaction to the mechanized society that had evolved in the United States. Many couples changed life-styles in a concern for the effects industrialization had caused on the environment. More simple styles of living resulted, along with a renewed interest in organic gardening, handcrafts, and basic skills.

Quilting also was viewed with renewed interest, which was heightened when many quilts were made to celebrate the Bicentennial in 1976. This quilt awakening strengthened as many companies emerged to provide publications and materials for today's quiltmaker. No longer do women need to make do with fabric scraps to construct quilts out of necessity. Instead, women carefully select fabrics of varying patterns and colors to satisfy their creative and artistic instincts. No longer is quilting an isolated endeavor to create bedcovers. Instead, women join with their sisters nationwide to attend seminars and conferences and to exhibit their work with pride.

CONTEMPORARY QUILTS IN THE TRADITIONAL STYLE

by Marsha McCloskey

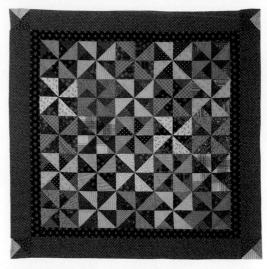

Whirlygig quilt top, made by Marsha McCloskey, 1986, Seattle, Washington, 52 1/2" x 52 1/2". Simple blocks set side by side create secondary and tertiary designs. Several fabrics in this top were overdyed at home with Rit® dye. (Collection of the artist)

Fabric Selection and Color

The first part of this book provides a short history of quiltmaking and textile production in the United States. By carefully studying examples of early quiltmakers' art, much can be learned about the character of patterns and fabrics that they used. Knowing why and when a particular fabric, pattern, or design style was used can provide helpful information in quiltmaking today.

What draws us to old quilts? Why are they exciting? Really look at the quilts pictured in this book. What are the colors? How are the prints used? In the old quilts, we see that early quilters routinely broke many of our present-day quilt-design "rules." Every kind of print was used, not just little flowers, but stripes, plaids, polka dots, and large florals as well. Colors rarely matched perfectly. Though design motifs were regularly repeated, the quilts were anything but static. Seemingly random and exuberant use of color and visual textures created sparkle and movement.

Quilters who came before us collected fabrics just like we do. Perhaps they did not have our economic resources, but they did buy, collect, save, and trade pretty pieces of cloth for their quilts. Types of fabrics accumulated depended on current levels of technology, fashion, and distribution systems. With a preference for cottons that would be easy to piece and quilt well, quilters chose the best quality cloth in the most durable colors. Some dyes were more trustworthy than others, and since fashion dictated fabric production somewhat, the color schemes of many quilts were pre-determined.

The color combinations used by early quiltmakers can serve as inspiration in our own color choices. Often certain colors indicate the era in which a quilt was made, such as the red and green quilts from the mid-19th century, dark prints from 1890—1925, and the pastels of the 1920s. Study the photos in the first section of this book to find color schemes that appeal to you.

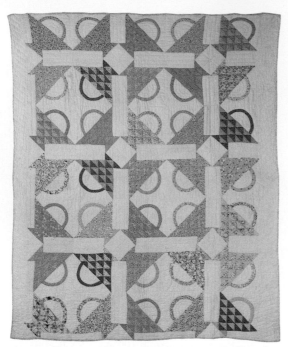

Cherry Basket, origin unknown, c. 1930, 71" x 84". Creating beauty while "making do", the maker of this quilt used flour sacks for the pastel prints and plain background fabrics. (Collection of Marsha McCloskey, Seattle, Washington)

The design style of many old quilts reflects the absence of large pieces of purchased yardage. These women were working from collections of scraps. In contrast to contemporary quilts, blocks often were set side by side without being separated by lattices or unpieced alternate blocks, which would require larger pieces of fabric. Side triangles of diagonally set designs often were filled with pieced half-blocks. If lattices or plain blocks were present, often the prints used in a given design space would change as the quilter used up a fabric and had to make do with another.

Many old quilts were pieced all the way to the binding and had no borders. To put a border on a quilt, after all, required fairly large pieces of uncut cloth that had to be purchased or woven for the purpose. Borders, when present, often were pieced or made of several different fabrics.

Although many old-time quilters used outline quilting (1/4" away from seams) or "in the ditch quilting" (hidden in the seams), overall quilting designs were also used. Overall quilting designs tie the quilt together rather than emphasizing the individual blocks.

Many straight-line and grid patterns developed because they were easy to mark and did not require quilting stencils. The Amish seemed to prefer a double row of stitches as an overall quilting pattern. A pattern called the Baptist Fan was very common. Drawn with a pencil on a string attached to a pivot point, this pattern was fast and easy to quilt since it followed the natural movement of the arm. Hanging Diamonds and Clamshell were also popular all-over quilting designs. Sometimes an early quiltmaker only needed to go to the cupboard for templates to trace. The Teacup and Dish patterns surely originated from tracing around the family china to form interlocking circles for quilting designs.

More intricate quilting designs required stencils for marking. There were homemade paper, cardboard, or tin stencils to trace around. There were also pierced-tin quilting stencils, where either cinnamon or cornstarch was rubbed over the openings (for marking on light or dark fabric), so each area could be quilted and the cornstarch or cinnamon brushed away.

Perforated-paper quilting patterns to be used with blue chalk were available during the 1930s, as well as stamped quilting patterns, which were ironed on fabric, leaving a design to be quilted.

Baptist Fan

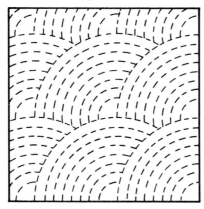

Clamshell

Hanging Diamonds

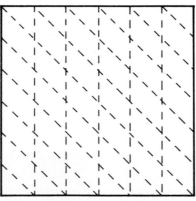

Teacup

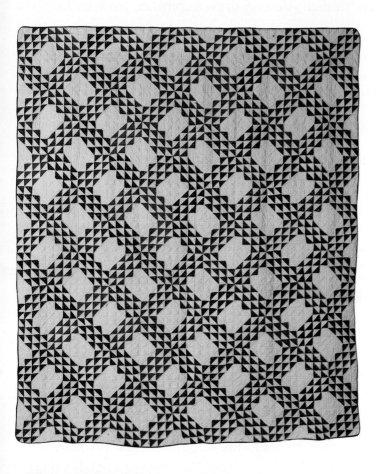

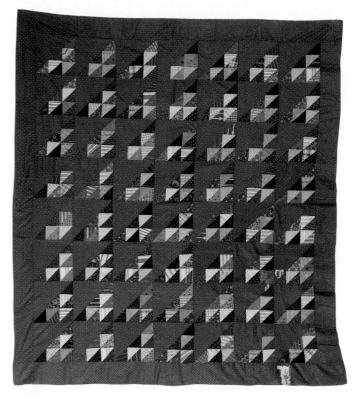

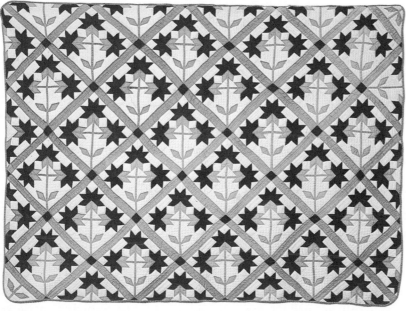

Ocean Waves, origin unknown, c. 1890, 72" x 82". Indigo dye was exceptionally durable. Many quilters during the 1800s used a blue and white color combination for their best work. (Collection of That Patchwork Place, Inc., Bothell, Washington)

Birds in the Air quilt top, made by Clara Countryman, Wyoming, Iowa, c. 1920, 70" x 81". The blue background fabric still has its label pasted to the border. (Collection of Dick and Nancy Dice, Bellevue, Washington)

Bed of Peonies, maker unknown, c. 1860, Kentucky, 67" x 90". Red, green and white was a popular color combination in the mid 1800s when reliable green dyes became available. Even so, many of the greens faded badly with time. (Collection of That Patchwork Place, Inc., Bothell, Washington)

The character of your quilt will depend on your own fabric collection and design choices. No other quilter has been where you have been, made the same choices, bought the same fabrics. Your collection and quilt knowledge are unique. Your quilts will be too, even though you may draw inspiration from quilts of the past.

To select your fabric begin with a color idea or theme. Though another quilt may inspire you, many times a fabric will provide the key inspiration for color in a quilt. This main fabric or idea print will give you color clues as to what other fabrics will go with it. Think in terms of related colors and contrasts. If your idea print is dark, choose something light in a related color to go with it. When two fabrics are side by side, there should be a definite line where one stops and the other begins. This shows contrast.

Contrast, both in color and visual texture, makes pieced designs more visible. Visual texture is the way a print looks—is it spotty, smooth, plain, dappled, linear, rhythmical, or swirly? Are the figures far apart or close together? Mix large prints with small prints, flowery all-over designs with linear and rhythmical prints. Too many similar prints can create a dull surface or one that is visually confusing.

Detail, **Churn Dash,** made by Marsha McCloskey. Plaids, stripes, polka dots, and large and small florals in pinks, rusts, browns and navies combine to make this contemporary quilt reminiscent of the 1800s.

Your fabric collection may need a little rounding out. Most of us have a preponderance of little flowery calicoes. When I recently evaluated my own fabric collection, I found it did not provide the full range of colors and visual textures that I felt necessary to work on multi-fabric quilts. I had no plaids, few stripes, and few really large prints. Following is a list of the types of prints to look for to make your collection more versatile.

1.   Plaids and checks. The most useful seem to be low-contrast designs with only two or three colors. Look for homespun, 100 percent cotton ginghams, checks and plaid shirtings. These linear designs add excitement and liveliness to a quilt design. Strong linear patterns lead the eye, give direction, and create motion.

2.   Geometrics. These are prints without flowers—linear designs usually associated with men's ties, pajamas, and boxer shorts.

3.   Polka dots. All kinds and sizes.

4.   Large multicolored prints. Look for paisleys and cabbage roses—large, finely etched figures that flow and have relatively low contrast between the colors.

5.   Simple stripes. Again, look for shirtings. Both fine and bold stripes are useful.

6.   Border stripes. These can provide many prints from the same cloth as well as give the linear quality, which can be so useful in a pieced design.

7.   Pictorial prints. Like the sport prints so popular during the late 1800s, these prints will add interest and charm to your quilt. Look for small, finely etched horses, ducks, boats, stars, acorns, flags, scissors, etc.

8. Large two-color prints. Look for low-contrast, finely etched two-color prints that flow. Both light and dark types are desirable. (Light ones are very rare.)

9. Quiet prints. Don't neglect this important category. These visually neutral prints will enable you to use the more busy and flamboyant prints successfully. Quiet prints are generally two-color prints with low contrast and a small all-over figure or linear design. Both light and dark tones are useful. Quiet prints in the neutral tones of gray, beige, and taupe can be added to color combinations without drastically changing them. Neutral prints and colors quiet or dilute busy print and color combinations.

An excellent resource on combining print fabrics is *Calico and Beyond: The Use of Patterned Fabric in Quilts* by Roberta Horton. She provides many helpful exercises in combining patterned fabrics.

For best results, select lightweight, closely woven, 100 percent cotton fabrics. Polyester content may make small patchwork pieces difficult to cut and sew accurately. Preshrink all fabrics before use. Wash light and dark colors separately with regular laundry detergent and warm water. If you suspect a dark color might run, rinse it separately in plain warm water until the water remains clear. Dry fabrics in the dryer and press them well before cutting.

The 100 percent cotton ideal is not always possible with quilts created from fabric collections of long-standing. Some of my most interesting prints were purchased before I followed the 100 percent rule—they are polyester/cotton blends of uncertain content. I know I shouldn't use them, but the colors and prints are unobtainable today and often serve a unique design purpose in the quilt—so I use them anyway.

As you dig through your fabrics, you will probably find some real uglies—high-contrast prints in harsh colors that just won't blend with softer, more sophisticated tones in your collection. Some garish problem prints can be toned down and made useable with simple home dyeing. Tea and coffee have long been used to lower contrast in busy prints, but commercial home dyes can be used as well. While deep colors won't be achieved this way, contrast within a print can be lowered and bright white spots changed to medium tones.

Consider home dyeing of fabrics in your collection to be wholly experimental and use due caution. Test your dyed fabrics in varying situations (exposure to sun, hot and cold water, etc.) before using them in quilts. Expect some failures. Some ugly fabrics just get worse. As a rule, 100 percent cottons take dye better than polyester blends, but don't let that stop you from trying. For the "dye pot" I choose only fabrics that I know I will not use in their present form. It is also prudent to dye only half of such a fabric, conserving the rest in its original form. Who knows, it might regain appeal at some later date or have some obscure archival value.

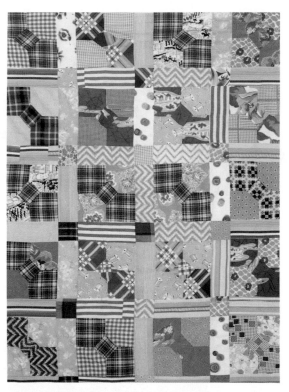

Detail, **Bow Tie** quilt top, origin unknown, c. 1930, 72" x 82". This hodgepodge of prints from the 1930s is a fascinating sampler of prints of the era. (Collection of Joyce Pennington, Edmonds, Washington)

69

Remember also that the effect of tannic acid in tea may prove harmful to fabrics over a long period of time, and that the effect of commercial dyes will not always be consistent. But an exercise in home dying is reminiscent of our pioneer sisters, who dyed most of their fabrics, and will help us develop an appreciation of their work.

A quilting group in Bellingham, Washington shared this home-dyeing method with me:

1. Use Rit® dye in powder or liquid form, following the instructions on the package.
2. Fill the washing machine to its lowest level with hot water. Add the dye (powdered crystals should be dissolved first in a small container of hot water).
3. Add 1/4 cup of detergent to the dye water to aid wicking—the absorption of the dye.
4. Place wet fabric in the dye water and run the washer through its full wash and rinse cycle. Run fabric through another cycle, only this time, add one quart of white vinegar to the wash cycle.

    1st wash—dye/detergent
    1st rinse—clear water
    2nd wash—vinegar
    2nd rinse—clear water

5. To test the fastness of the dye, sew some of the dyed fabric to muslin and wash as you would your quilt. When I did this, there was a little dye loss, but the colors did not run onto the muslin.

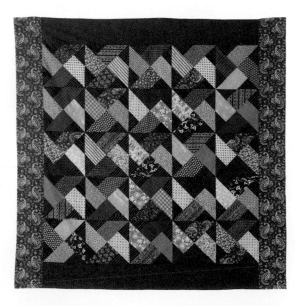

Waterwheel quilt top, made by Marsha McCloskey, 1986, Seattle, Washington, 49 1/2" x 49 1/2". Here, a simple old-fashioned block is repeated in a color recipe of many fabrics to create an overall design with a contemporary look. (Collection of the artist)

Designing Your Quilt

From studying the quilts in this book, you probably have a good idea of the type of quilt you want to make. The easiest way to proceed is to use an existing block pattern and quilt plan. There are 18 complete plans provided in the third section of this book. These plans include templates, color suggestions, fabric requirements, and step-by-step instructions. If you prefer to create your own quilt designs, use the following guidelines and arrange your blocks in one of the set plans given with the 12" block patterns.

What follows here is a description of the process I use to create quilt tops pieced from many fabrics. It is a "design-as-you-go" process employed by many quilters. The steps are simple, the process engrossing. Read the section over. Start your quilt from scratch as described here or incorporate some of the suggestions in the quilt designs provided later in the book.

For scrap or multi-fabric quilts, sometimes the most simple block designs are the easiest to work with and the most successful. They are the types of blocks that old-time quiltmakers would have chosen to use up scraps and get a quilt made in as little time as possible. Many such simple block patterns are provided in the pattern section of this book.

Waterwheel and Whirlygig are patterns often passed over as being just too plain to spend time on. Yet, when set together side by side and done in a many-fabric recipe, these blocks create secondary and tertiary designs over the quilt surface, which change and move and demand attention. These lowly blocks make truly respectable, even exciting quilt designs.

Choosing a simple block design allows the work to go quickly. Making a few sample blocks of these designs takes so little time, especially on the sewing machine, that you will want to try out more colors and more fabrics just to see how they will turn out.

Start with a line drawing of a potential block design. Shade it in, experimenting with different arrangements of light, medium, and dark tones. Most old-time block designs can be made with two or three basic values—light and dark or light, medium, and dark. Keep in mind that these are relative terms. How a fabric is defined depends on the fabrics around it. Medium tones are especially changeable. They can be light when placed next to a dark fabric or dark when put beside a very light one.

Next draw four or more blocks together. Study the new line drawing. What do you see? Is another design created where the blocks meet? Can these secondary forms be emphasized with new shading? Sketch until you develop a light and dark relationship that seems to work. Then try it with fabric.

Define a color recipe for your design. What color will be the dark? What the light? A simple recipe would be to have a constant background fabric in all the blocks and to make the design motif in different scrap fabrics. Another recipe would be to change the background fabric in each block as well. This inconsistency adds depth and movement to the simplest quilt designs. (See Churn Dash, Clay's Choice and 54-40 or Fight.)

The color recipe for Waterwheel was to make all the small background triangles with the same dark green fabric and the "blades" with medium red tones going one direction and beige to gold light tones going the other.

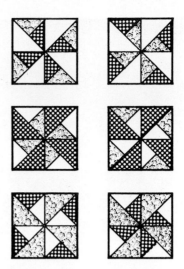

Determine light, medium, & dark areas in a design with a few quick sketches.

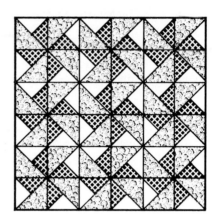

Having chosen a tentative color recipe based on your color theme and shaded sketches, choose a range of fabrics for each color group in the recipe. If black is one of the colors, pick several black prints in differing intensities and visual textures. Pull every black in your collection that even remotely fits the criteria. Not all of these prints will be used, but it is important to study the possibilities. Do the same with each color group in the recipe.

Resist overmatching colors and textures. Use all types of prints. As a color group, reds can range from rust to red to maroon to brown and still occupy the same position in the block design. A group of lights can go from very white to ecru to medium tones. Darks can range from very dark to medium. If your color grouping looks boring, throw in a color surprise, a nonsequitur—navy in a run of browns or true red where only shades of maroon and rust have been used.

Color Recipe for Waterwheel

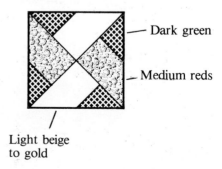

— Dark green

— Medium reds

Light beige to gold

Churn Dash, made by Marsha McCloskey, 1985, Seattle, Washington, 41 1/2" x 50". High and low contrast design blocks set with alternate blocks of several different fabrics give interest and movement beyond the simple quilt design. (Collection of the artist)

Sister's Choice, made by Marsha McCloskey, 1982, Seattle, Washington, 42" x 53". Consistent lattice treatment and repeated block motifs visually hold this multi-fabric quilt design together (Collection of the artist)

Once you have chosen a block design, an arrangement of lights and darks, and pulled runs of fabric from your collection, the next step is to make a fabric sketch. This trial run of blocks will test your color recipe, the projected color arrangement.

Cut the pieces for four or more blocks from your chosen fabrics. Place the shapes on a piece of needlepunch or flannel hung on the wall to evaluate the effect. Cut more pieces and make changes until it pleases you. When the color arrangment is set, piece the blocks. Now, cut and sew more blocks in the same recipe. Make needed color and design changes as the quilt grows.

Feel free to experiment with different prints and color arrangements. Push yourself. Be adventurous. Go beyond what you consider safe fabric and color usage. Break a few rules. Forget about centering large motifs; cabbage roses and other large prints work better cut randomly anyway. Stripes and plaids can be cut randomly, too—even off grain if you wish. Try using the wrong side of some prints to get just the right tone. If you make a mistake in piecing, consider leaving it in to create interest. If you run out of one fabric, substitute another and keep going.

One strategy for making quilts more interesting visually is to vary the contrast in the unit blocks. High contrast blocks are needed to establish the design, but more interest will be created when other blocks in the quilt have lower contrast. A good example is the Churn Dash quilt shown here. It's okay to lose the design in some parts of the quilt. The viewer expects the same design to be regularly repeated and will search for a "disappearing" design motif to make sure it is there.

Background fabrics are particularly important in creating variations in the contrast of the blocks. Bright whites can hold the same design spaces in blocks as ecru and more medium tones. The whites will add sparkle to the quilt and lead the eye from one part to the next. Yellow, used in small amounts is, like bright white, a real eyecatcher, creating movement wherever it appears.

Before the blocks are sewn together, try out several block arrangements or sets. Blocks can be set straight-on or on the diagonal. Some look best side by side. Others look best separated by alternate blocks or lattices. Take time to play with your blocks and arrange them in different ways. Original quilt plans sometimes need changing and you are the one to make the judgment. Vary spatial relationships. Think about borders—does the quilt need them? Even though many old quilts didn't have them, we can make our own decisions.

The coloring of the set pieces, alternate blocks, or lattices is a very important part of the quilt's total look. Set pieces that are the same color as the background of the unit blocks will float the design, while those cut from contrasting fabric will outline each block and emphasize its squareness.

A quilt-in-progress needs constant reevaluation. Don't, however, let the endless possibilities and decisions paralyze you. At some point, just sew the top together and get on with it.

SMALL QUILT BLOCKS

There are patterns and quilt plans using the eight small quilt blocks in this section of the book: Broken Dishes, Cake Stand, Churn Dash, Double Ninepatch, Double Ninepatch with Pieced Lattice, Sawtooth Star, Snowball, and Underground Railway. The blocks range in size from 6'' to 9'', and are used for both wall hangings and full-size quilts.

The quilts share templates, lattice and set pieces which are found on page 82-85 of this section. Yardage, dimensions, complete directions and diagrams, and templates are given for each quilt. Measurements for patterns and borders include 1/4'' seam allowance. Cutting directions are for one block only; multiply them by the number of blocks you are making to determine complete cutting specifications. Cutting directions for set pieces, lattices and pieced borders are for the entire quilt.

Templates have seam lines, (broken lines) as well as, cutting lines (solid lines). Grain-lines are for the lengthwise or crosswise grain and are shown with an arrow on each piece.

Fold lines indicate where half templates are given due to space limitations. Complete the other half of the pattern when you make templates. In some cases, smaller pieces overlap larger pieces, so be sure to include the entire template, including the space covered by the smaller piece, when you make the larger templates.

Consult the Glossary of Techniques on pages 145-150 for complete directions on quiltmaking techniques.

BROKEN DISHES

9" block

Measurements for patterns and borders include 1/4" seam allowance.

Materials: 45" wide yardage
Light fabric: 3/4 yd. muslin
Dark print: 1/2 yd. assorted brown scraps
Backing: 7/8 yd.
Batting, binding, and thread to finish

Cutting:
B: Cut 20 light
    Cut 20 dark
F: Cut 4 light
Sawtooth Border: Using Template B, cut 52 light
    and 52 dark

Piecing Diagram

Make 4

Make 5

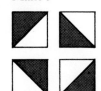

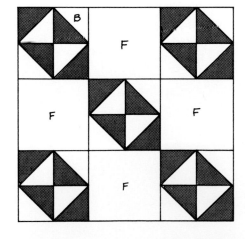

Dimensions: 34" x 34"
(Color photo, page 35)

Directions:
1. Cut borders from light fabric:
   For Outside Border cut two strips 3 1/2" x 28 1/2" and two strips 3 1/2" x 34"
   For Inside Border cut two strips 3 1/2" x 18 1/2" and two strips 3 1/2" x 24 1/2"
2. Cut and piece 4 "Broken Dishes" blocks.
3. Set together blocks as shown.
4. Add 3 1/2" x 18 1/2" borders to top and bottom.
5. Stitch 3 1/2" x 24 1/2" borders to sides.
6. Piece a 12 unit Sawtooth Border segment for each side using photograph as a guide for placement. Add Corner Sawtooth Unit to each end of two Border Segments.
7. Add Sawtooth Border Segments to top and bottom of quilt top. Stitch Sawtooth Border Segments with Corner Sawtooth Units to sides of quilt top.
8. Add 3 1/2" x 28 1/2" borders to top and bottom.
9. Stitch 3 1/2" x 34" borders to sides.
10. Add batting and backing, then quilt or tie. Quilting suggestion: Quilt a grid through the Broken Dishes blocks and a cable design in each muslin border. Quilt inside each triangle of Sawtooth Border.
11. Bind with bias strips.

Note: Use the Bias-Strip Piecing technique given on page 147 to quickly piece the triangles.
Use Template G.

CAKE STAND©

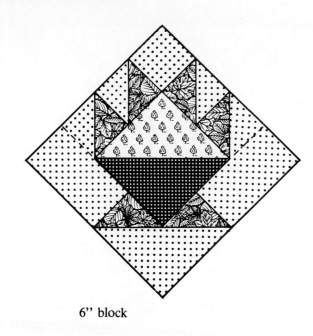

6" block

Measurements for patterns and borders include 1/4" seam allowance.

Materials: 45" wide yardage
Light print: 2 yds. assorted scraps
Dark print: 4 yds. assorted brown scraps
Accent: 3/4 yd. assorted red scraps
Backing: 4 3/8 yds. fabric
Batting, binding, and thread to finish

Cutting:

A: Cut 2 light
B: Cut 6 accent
   Cut 4 light
C: Cut 1 dark
   Cut 2 light
D: Cut 1 light
Set Piece 1: Cut 4 dark
Set Piece 2: Cut 32 dark
Set Piece 3: Cut 63 dark

Piecing Diagram

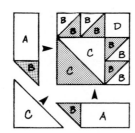

Note: Use the Bias-Strip Piecing technique given on page 147 to quickly piece the triangles.

Use Template D.

© Marsha McCloskey, 1983

Dimensions: 85" x 75"
(Color photo, page 32)

Directions:

1. This quilt has alternating pieced and solid borders. Cut 2 border strips, each 2 1/2" x 75 1/2" from dark fabric for solid borders.
2. Cut and piece 80 "Cake Stand" blocks.
3. Join blocks and set pieces as shown.
4. Add pieced border segment to top and bottom.
5. Add solid border to top and bottom.
6. Add additional pieced border segment to bottom.
7. Add batting and backing, then quilt or tie. Quilting suggestion: Use the Amish double row of stitches horizontally across quilt top.
8. Bind with bias strips.

Border Segment

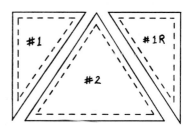

Pieced Border
For each segment:
#1 + 1R: Cut 1 each from accent
#2: Cut 59 accent
    Cut 60 light

1. Piece a segment of 59 accent pieces #2 and 60 light pieces #2.
2. Add #1 + #1R cut from accent to each end of segment.

CHURN DASH ©

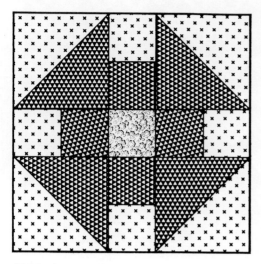

6" block

Measurements for patterns and borders include 1/4" seam allowance.

Materials: 45" wide yardage

    Light print: 3/8 yd. pinks for background

    Dark print: 1/2 yd. assorted brown and blue scraps

    Accent color: 1/4 yd. assorted brown and blue scraps

    Set pieces: 1 yd. assorted tan prints

    Border stripe: 1 1/2 yds.

    Backing: 1 1/2 yds.

    Batting, binding, and thread to finish

Cutting:

    J: Cut 4 light

          Cut 4 dark

    I: Cut 4 light

          Cut 4 dark

          Cut 1 accent

    Set piece 1: Cut 4 tan

    Set piece 2: Cut 14 tan

    Set Piece 3: Cut 12 tan

Piecing Diagram

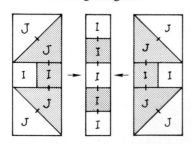

© Marsha McCloskey, 1982

Dimensions: 41 1/2" x 50"
(Color photo, page 72)

Directions:

1. This quilt has a single border of striped fabric. Cut two border strips 4 1/2" x 42". Cut two border strips 4 1/2" x 50 1/2".
2. Cut and piece 20 "Churn Dash" blocks.
3. Join blocks and set pieces as shown.
4. Add borders.
5. Add batting and backing, then quilt or tie. Quilting suggestion: Use a fan quilting pattern to unify the quilt surface.
6. Bind with bias strips.

Assembly Sequence

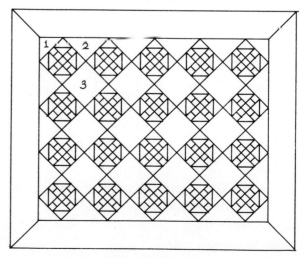

DOUBLE NINEPATCH

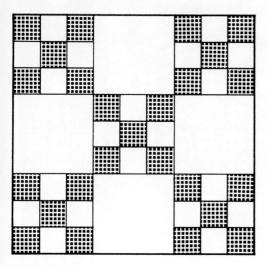

9" block

Measurements for patterns and borders include 1/4" seam allowance.

Materials: 45" wide yardage
Light print: 4 1/2 yds. for background
Dark print: 1 3/4 yds.
Backing: 4 1/2 yds.
Batting, binding, and thread to finish

Cutting:
E: Cut 20 light
     Cut 25 dark
F: Cut 4 light
Set piece 4: Cut 22 light
Set piece 5: Cut 4 light
Set Block: Cut 30 squares 9 1/2" x 9 1/2" from
     light

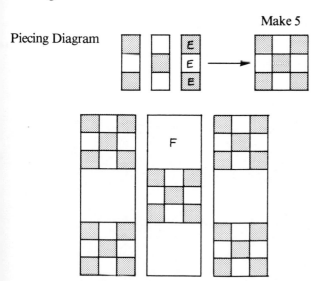

Piecing Diagram   Make 5

Note: Use the Strip Piecing technique given on page 146 to quickly piece the Ninepatch blocks.

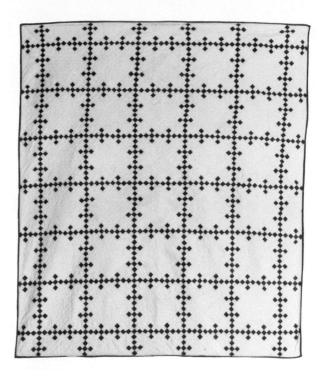

Dimensions: 76 1/2" x 89"
(Color photo, page 14)

Directions:
1. Cut and piece 42 "Double Ninepatch" blocks.
2. Join blocks and set pieces as shown.
3. Add batting and backing, then quilt or tie as you wish.
    Quilting suggestion: A double row of horizontal lines was used on this antique quilt.
4. Bind with bias strips of dark fabric.

Assembly Sequence

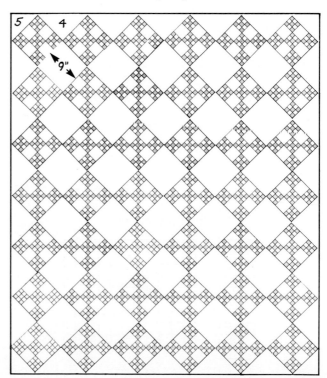

77

DOUBLE NINEPATCH WITH PIECED LATTICE

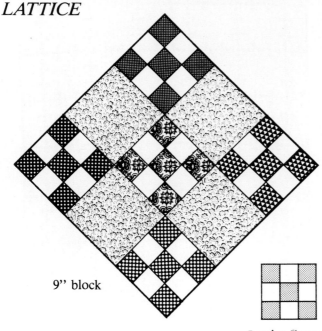

9" block

Lattice Square

Measurements for patterns and borders include 1/4" seam allowance.

Materials: 45" wide yardage

Light fabric: 3/4 yd. muslin
Medium print: 1 yd. assorted scraps
Accent print: 1 1/4 yds. deep red
Dark fabric: 1 yd. navy for lattice strips and set piece 6.

Cutting:

E: Cut 25 medium
    Cut 20 light
F: Cut 4 accent
Lattice squares: Cut 5 medium
                 Cut 4 light
Lattice pieces: Cut 24 dark strips, 3 1/2" x 9 1/2"
Set piece 2: Cut 10 accent
Set piece 5: Cut 4 accent
Set piece 6: Cut 20 dark

Dimensions: 45 1/2" x 64"
(Color photo, page 15)

Directions:

1. Cut and piece 18 "Double Ninepatch" blocks.
2. Cut and piece 18 lattice squares.
3. Join blocks, lattice squares, lattice pieces and set pieces as shown.
4. Add batting and backing, quilt or tie.
   Quilting suggestion: use a double row of stitches horizontally across the quilt top.
5. Bind with bias strips.

Assembly Sequence

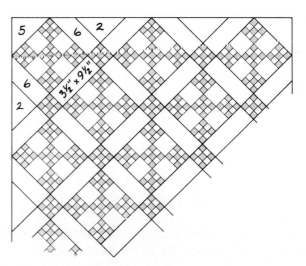

Piecing Diagram

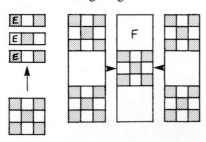

SAWTOOTH STAR

6" block

Measurements for patterns and borders include 1/4" seam allowance.

Materials: 45" wide yardage
Light fabric: 2 yds.
Dark fabric: 1/8 yd. each of 30 different prints
Backing: 1 5/8 yds.
Batting, binding, and thread to finish

Cutting:
B: Cut 8 dark
    Cut 8 light
D: Cut 4 light
F: Cut 1 dark
Set Piece 1: Cut 4 light
Set Piece 2: Cut 18 light
Set Piece 3: Cut 20 light

Piecing Diagram

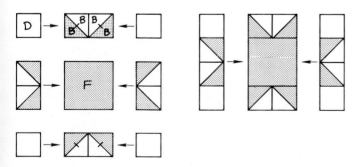

Note: Use the Bias-Strip Piecing technique given on page 147 to quickly piece the triangles.
Use Template D.

Dimensions: 42 1/2" x 51"
(Color photo, page 19)

Directions:
1. Cut and piece 30 "Sawtooth Star" blocks.
2. Join blocks and set pieces as shown.
3. Add batting and backing, then quilt or tie as you wish.
   Quilting suggestion: Quilt feathered wreaths in the alternate plain blocks.
4. Bind with bias strips of dark fabric.

Assembly Sequence

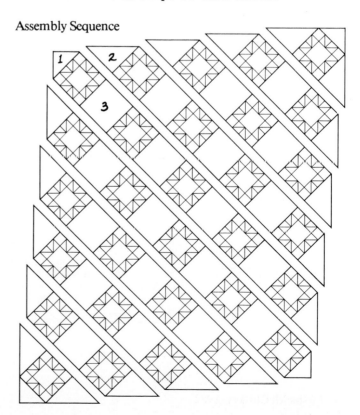

SNOWBALL©

"Snowball" is an allover design created when two different unit blocks are set in a checkerboard fashion on the diagonal. Use assorted scrap fabrics.

Ninepatch, 6"

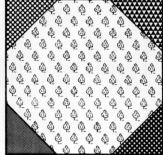

Snowball, 6"

Measurements for patterns and borders include 1/4" seam allowance.

Materials: 45" wide yardage

Light print: 1 3/4 yds. for background, set pieces, and binding.

Dark prints: 1/2 yds. assorted scraps

Backing: 1 3/4 yds. fabric.

Batting, binding, and thread to finish

Cutting:

Ninepatch Block: Cut 9 G from assorted scraps

Snowball Block: Cut 1 K from light print
                   Cut 4 H from assorted scraps

Set piece 1: Cut 4 from light print

Set piece 2: Cut 14 from light print

Piecing Diagram

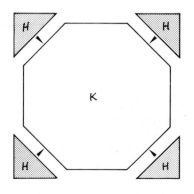

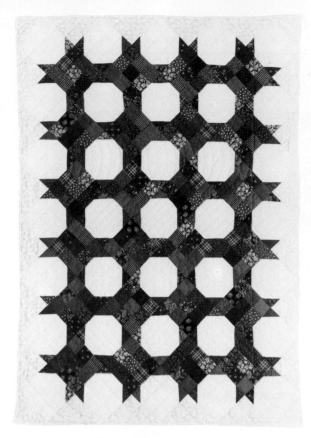

Dimensions: 40" x 58"

(Color photo, page 3)

Directions:

1. Cut and piece 35 "Snowball" blocks.
2. Cut and piece 24 "Ninepatch" blocks from scraps.
3. Join blocks and set pieces together as shown.
4. Add batting and backing, then quilt or tie. Quilting suggestion: Divide the quilt into areas, using a different grid or quilting pattern in each area.
5. Bind with bias strips.

Assembly Sequence

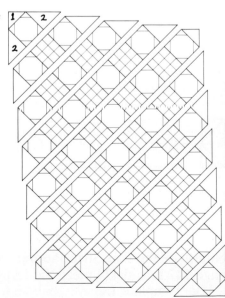

© Marsha McCloskey, 1982

UNDERGROUND RAILWAY ©

6" block

Lattice square

Measurements for patterns and borders include 1/4" seam allowance.

Materials: 45" wide yardage

Light fabric: 1 1/2 yds. for background and first border.

Dark print: 1 1/4 yds. for blocks and outside border.

Medium solid: 3/8 yd.

Backing: 1 1/2 yds.

Batting, binding, and thread to finish

Dimensions: 42" x 51" (Color photo, page 64)

Directions:

1. Cut border strips. Sew them together to form border units.
   From light print fabric:
   Cut two 2" x 42 1/2" strips
   Cut two 2" x 51 1/2" strips
   From dark print fabric:
   Cut two 5" x 42 1/2" strips
   Cut two 5" x 51 1/2" strips

2. Cut and piece 12 "Underground Railway" blocks and 20 lattice squares.

3. Set together blocks, lattice pieces (#7) and lattice squares as shown. Add borders and miter corners.

4. Add batting and backing, then quilt or tie. Quilting suggestion: Quilt diagonal rows across quilt top, with diagonal rows in the opposite direction across border. Bind with bias strips.

Cutting:

C: Cut 2 light
    Cut 2 dark

D: Cut 4 light
    Cut 4 medium

Lattice squares:

D: Cut 2 light
    Cut 2 medium

Set piece #7: Cut 31 light

Piecing Diagram

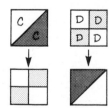

Note: Use the Strip Piecing technique given on page 146 to quickly piece the Four Patch blocks.

© Marsha McCloskey, 1982

Assembly Sequence

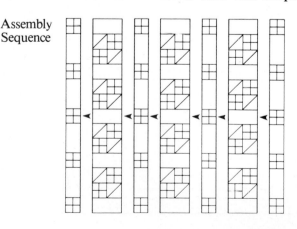

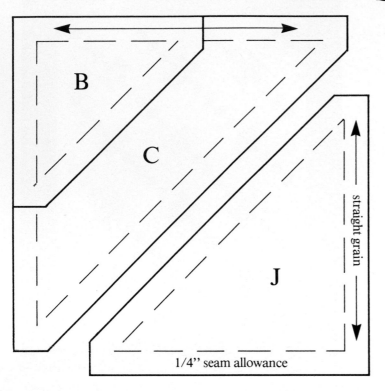

B

C

J

straight grain

1/4" seam allowance

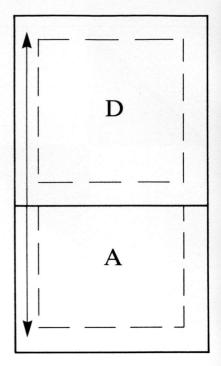

D

A

NOTE: Smaller pieces overlap larger pieces, so be sure to include the entire template, including the space covered by the smaller piece, when you make the larger template.

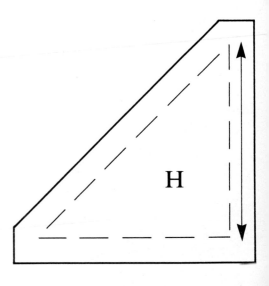

H

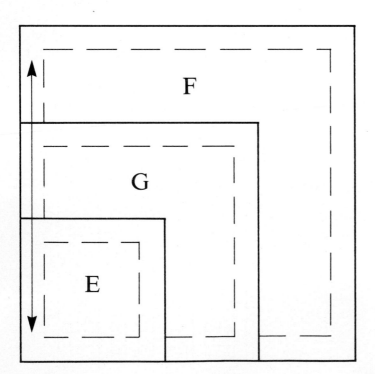

F

G

E

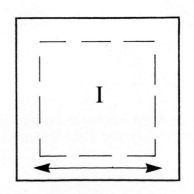

I

SET PIECES - SMALL QUILT BLOCKS

NOTE: Smaller pieces overlap larger pieces, so be sure to include the entire template, including the space covered by the smaller piece, when you make the larger template.

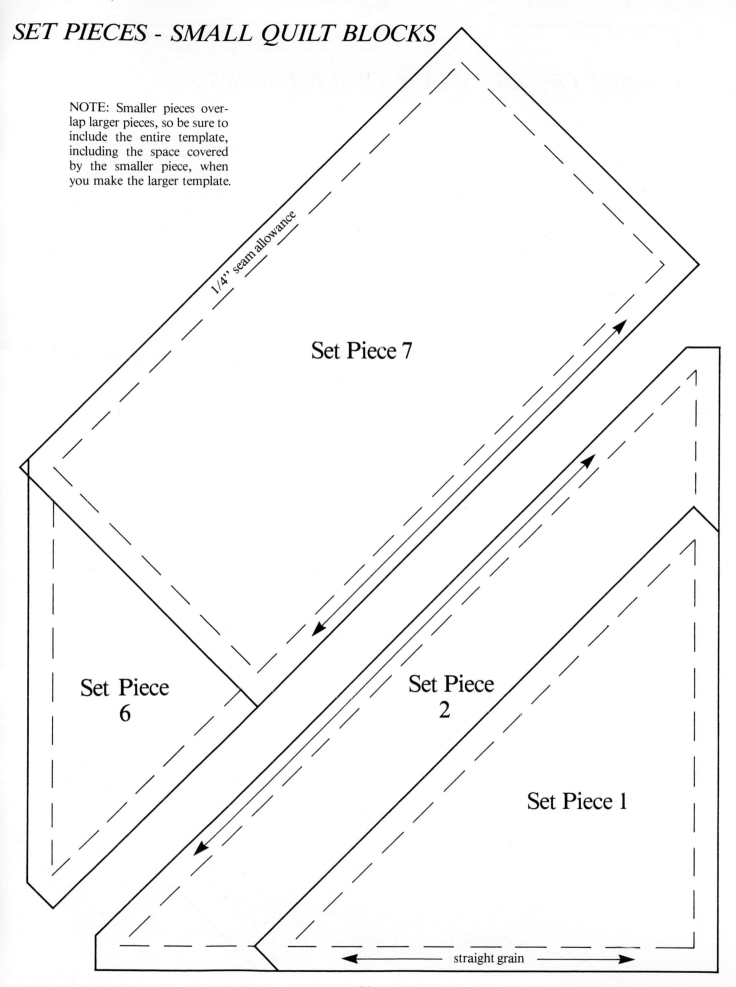

1/4" seam allowance

Set Piece 7

Set Piece 6

Set Piece 2

Set Piece 1

straight grain

SET PIECES - SMALL QUILT BLOCKS

Set Piece 3

1/4'' seam allowance

fold

K

straight grain

SET PIECES - SMALL QUILT BLOCKS

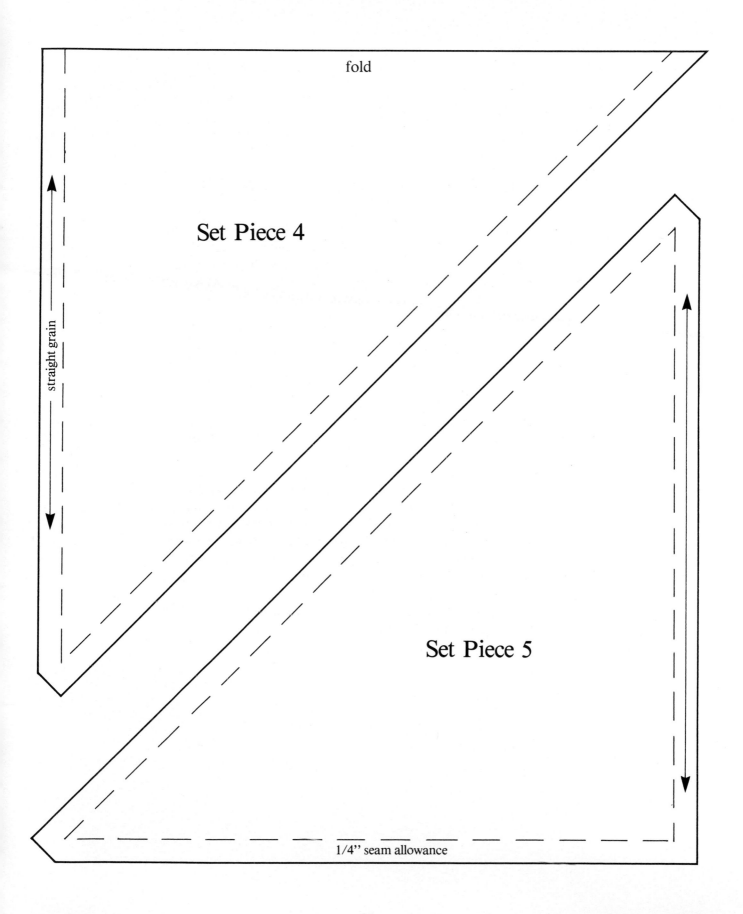

fold

straight grain

Set Piece 4

Set Piece 5

1/4" seam allowance

EIGHT INCH QUILT BLOCKS

There are patterns for ten 8" quilt blocks in this section of the book: Basket, Clay's Choice, 54-40 or Fight, Four Patch, Gentleman's Fancy, Hovering Hawks, Road to California, Sister's Choice, Waterwheel and Whirlygig. Quilt plans are provided for each block and any block can easily be substituted in another setting since all the quilt plans accommodate 8" blocks.

The quilts share templates, lattice and set pieces which are found on page 97-101 of this section. Yardage, dimensions, complete directions and diagrams, and templates are provided for each quilt. Measurements for patterns and borders include 1/4" seam allowance. Cutting directions are for one block only; multiply them by the number of blocks to determine complete cutting specifications. Cutting directions for set pieces and lattices are for the entire quilt.

Templates have seam lines (broken lines) as well as cutting lines (solid lines). Grainlines are for the lengthwise or crosswise grain and are shown with an arrow on each piece. Fold lines indicate where half templates are given due to space limitations. Complete the other half of the pattern when you make templates. In some cases, smaller pieces overlap larger pieces, so be sure to include the entire template, including the space covered by the smaller piece when you make the larger templates.

Consult the Glossary of Techniques on pages 145-150 for complete directions on quiltmaking techniques.

BASKET ©

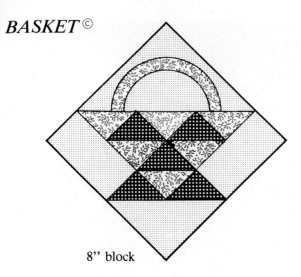

8" block

Measurements for patterns and borders include 1/4" seam allowance.

Materials: 45" wide yardage
  Light print: 1 3/4 yds. for background.
  Solid: 1/4 yd. pink
  Dark print: 3/4 yd. assorted pink scraps.
  Backing: 1 3/4 yds.
  Batting, binding, and thread to finish
Note: Use the Bias-Strip Piecing technique given on page 147 to quickly piece the triangles of the basket and Sawtooth border. Usc Template L.

Cutting:
  E: Cut 5 solid
      Cut 6 dark print
  B: Cut 1 light print from background
  P: Cut 2 light print from background
  T: Cut 1 light print background
  S: Cut 1 dark print to match basket
  Set Piece 1: Cut 6 light print
  Set Piece 2: Cut 4 light print
  Set Piece 3: Cut 10 light print
  Sawtooth Border:
  E: Cut 84 light print
      Cut 84 assorted dark prints
  L: Cut 4 light print

Piecing Diagram   T - background
                         S - handle

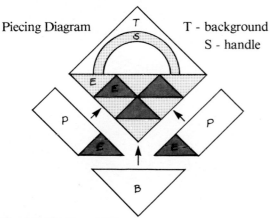

©Marsha McCloskey, 1983

Dimensions: 42 x 54"
  (Color photo, page 32)

Directions:

1. Cut borders from light fabric.
    For Outside Border cut two strips 2 1/2" x 52 1/2" and two strips 2 1/2" x 44".
    For Inside Border cut two strips 1 1/2" x 48 1/2" and two strips 2 1/2" x 34".
2. Cut and piece 12 "Basket" blocks.
3. Set together blocks and set pieces as shown.
4. Add 2 1/2" x 34" borders to top and bottom.
5. Stitch 1 1/2" x 48 1/2" borders to sides.
6. Piece an 18-unit Sawtooth Border for top and bottom.
    Piece a 24-unit Sawtooth Border segment for each side.
    Add Template L piece to each end of side borders.
7. Add Sawtooth Border segments to top and bottom of quilt top. Stitch Sawtooth Border segments with corner squares to sides of quilt top.
8. Add two strips 2 1/2" x 48 1/2" to sides.
9. Stitch two strips 2 1/2" x 52 1/2" strips to sides of quilt top.
10. Add two 2 1/2" x 44" strips to top and bottom.
11. Add batting and backing, then quilt or tie.
    Quilting suggestion: Use a fan quilting pattern to unify the quilt's surface.
12. Bind with bias strips.

CLAY'S CHOICE ©

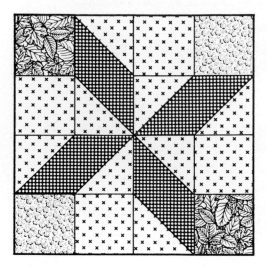

8" block

Measurements for patterns and borders include 1/4" seam allowance.

Materials: 45" wide yardage
Light print: 1/2 yd. assorted scraps
Medium print: 1/4 yd. assorted pink scraps
Accent print: 1/4 yd. assorted brown scraps
Dark print: 1/2 yd. assorted navy scraps for blocks and lattices
Borders: 3/4 yd. assorted medium and dark prints
Backing: 1 1/2 yds.
Batting, binding, and thread to finish

Cutting:
L: Cut 4 light
    Cut 2 medium
    Cut 2 accent
F: Cut 4 dark
A: Cut 8 light
Set pieces:
Template L: Cut 6 medium for lattice squares
Set Piece 6: Cut 17 dark for lattice

Piecing Diagram

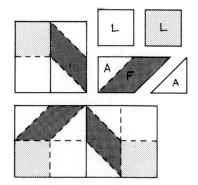

© Marsha McCloskey, 1986

Dimensions: 36" x 48"
(Color photo, page 24)

Directions:
1. Cut borders from medium and dark fabric:
   Cut 2 strips 5" x 28 1/2" from dark fabric
   Cut and piece 2 strips 5" x 48" from medium fabric
2. Cut and piece 12 "Clay's Choice" blocks.
3. Join blocks and set pieces as shown.
4. Add 5" x 28 1/2" borders to top and bottom.
5. Stitch 5" x 48" borders to sides.
6. Add batting and backing, then quilt or tie. Quilting suggestion: Divide the quilt into fourths and quilt each area with diagonal lines. Change direction of diagonal on each area and at borders.
7. Bind with bias strips.

DIVERSION ©

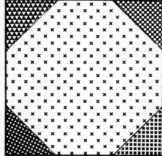

Diversion 8"   Snowball 8"

Measurements for patterns and borders include 1/4" seam allowance.

Materials: 45" wide yardage
   Light print: 1 1/2 yds. assorted light scraps
   Dark prints: 5/8 yd. assorted black scraps
   Medium prints: 1/2 yd. assorted red scraps
   Border fabric: 1 5/8 yds. medium print
   Backing: 3 1/4 yds.
   Batting, binding, and thread to finish

Cutting for "Gentleman's Fancy" block:
   Q. Cut 1 from medium print
   N: Cut 8 from dark prints
   C: Cut 8 from light prints
        Cut 4 from medium prints

Cutting for "Snowball" block:
   R: Cut 1 from light prints
   N: Cut 4 from medium prints
   Set Piece 2: Cut 4 from light
   Set Piece 8: Cut 12 from light
   Template C: Cut 12 from medium prints

Dimensions: 55 1/4" x 55 1/4"
(Color photo, page 4)

Directions:
1. Cut borders from medium print fabric:
      Cut 2 strips 5 1/2" x 45 3/4"
      Cut 2 strips 5 1/2" x 55 1/2"
2. Cut and piece 16 "Gentleman's Fancy" blocks.
3. Cut and piece 9 "Snowball" blocks as alternate blocks. Complete Set piece 8 by stitching Template N to corner to form point.
4. Join blocks and set pieces as shown.
5. Add 5 1/2" x 45 3/4" side borders.
6. Stitch 5 1/2" x 55 1/2" borders to top and bottom.
7. Add batting and backing, then quilt or tie. Quilting suggestion: Trace around a 7 1/2" diameter plate to form an overall quilting pattern.
8. Bind with bias strips.

Piecing Diagram

Make 4

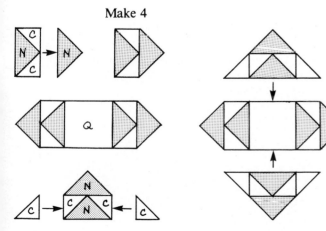

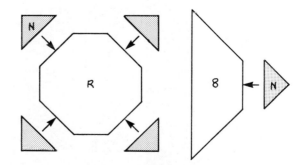

© Marsha McCloskey, 1984

54-40 OR FIGHT ©

8" block

Measurements for patterns and borders include 1/4" seam allowance.

Materials: 45" wide yardage

Light print: 1/2 yd. assorted gray scraps

Dark print: 1 yd. assorted black prints for background and lattices

Medium prints: 1/2 yd. assorted maroon scraps
1/4 yd. assorted light green scraps

Borders: 1/2 yd. assorted black prints
1/4 yd. maroon print

Backing: 1 1/2 yd.

Batting, binding, and thread to finish

Cutting:

I: Cut 4 light
IR: Cut 4 light
J: Cut 4 dark
K: Cut 8 dark
     Cut 6 maroon
     Cut 6 light green
     Set Piece 7: Cut 31 from assorted blacks
     Lattice square K: Cut 20 light green

Piecing Diagram

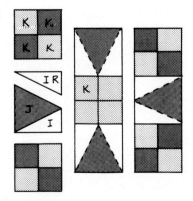

© Marsha McCloskey, 1986

Dimensions: 39" x 49"
(Color photo, page 24)

Directions:

1. This quilt has straight borders from pieced and print fabrics:
   Cut and piece two 3 1/2" x 29 3/4" borders from assorted black fabrics.
   Cut two 5" x 44 1/2" borders from black print fabric.
   Cut two 2 1/2" x 39" borders from maroon fabric.
2. Cut and piece 12 "54-40 or Fight" blocks.
3. Set pieced blocks together with Set pieces 7 and Lattice squares K as shown.
4. Add 3 1/2" x 29 3/4" pieced border to top and bottom.
5. Stitch 5" x 44 1/2" border to sides.
6. Add 2 1/2" x 39" border to top and bottom.
7. Add batting and backing, then quilt or tie.
8. Bind with bias strips.

Note: Use the Strip Piecing technique given on page 146 to quickly piece the Four Patch blocks.

90

FOUR PATCH

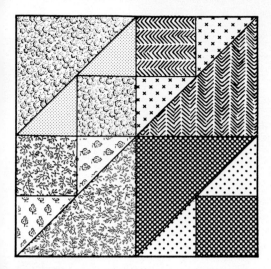

8" block

Dimensions: 52" x 60"
(Color photo, page 52)

Measurements for patterns and borders include 1/4" seam allowance.

Materials: 45" wide yardage
  Light print: 1 1/2 yds. assorted scraps
  Dark print; 3 yds. assorted scraps
  Borders: 1 5/8 yds.
  Backing: 3 yds.
  Batting, binding, and thread to finish

Cutting:
  A: Cut 8 light
  B: Cut 4 dark
  L: Cut 4 dark
      Cut 4 L for corner squares

Directions:

1. Cut and piece 36 "Four Patch" blocks.
2. Cut and piece 6 blocks for the middle row. Set together as shown.

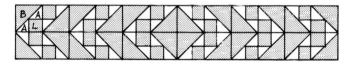

3. Join blocks as shown in a "barnraising set".
4. Add 2 1/2" x 56 1/2" borders to sides.
5. Join corner square L to each end of 2 1/2" x 48 1/2" top and bottom borders.
6. Stitch top and bottom borders with corner squares to quilt top.
7. Add batting and backing, then quilt or tie.
8. Bind with bias strips.

Piecing Diagram

Make 168

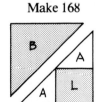

Make 36

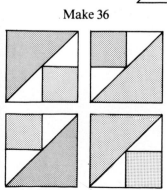

Make 6

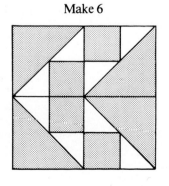

HOVERING HAWKS ©

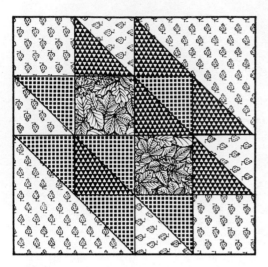

8" block

Measurements for patterns and borders include 1/4" seam allowance.

Materials: 45" wide yardage

Light print: 1/2 yd. assorted tan, beige and taupe scraps

Dark print: 1/2 yd. assorted brown scraps

Medium print: 1/2 yd. assorted blue and green scraps

Accent print: 1/4 yd. assorted scraps

Border: 1/2 yd. solid fabric

Backing: 7/8 yd.

Batting, binding, and thread to finish

Cutting:

A: Cut 4 light
    Cut 6 medium
    Cut 6 dark
B: Cut 2 light
L: Cut 2 light
    Cut 2 accent

Piecing Diagram

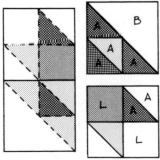

Dimensions: 30" x 30"
(Color photo, page 38)

Directions:

1. Cut borders from solid fabric:
     Cut 2 strips 3" x 24 1/2"
     Cut 2 strips 3" x 30"
2. Cut and piece 9 "Hovering Hawks" blocks.
3. Join blocks as shown.
4. Add 3" x 24 1/2" side borders.
5. Stitch 3" x 30" borders to top and bottom.
6. Add batting and backing, then quilt or tie. Quilting suggestion: Divide the quilt and borders into separate areas, using a different grid or quilting pattern in each area. Use a narrow cable on a portion of the border.
7. Bind with bias strips.

Note: Use the Bias-Strip Piecing technique given on page 147 to quickly piece the triangles.

Use Template L.

ROAD TO CALIFORNIA ©

8" block

Measurements for patterns and borders include 1/4" seam allowance.

Materials: 45" wide yardage
Light print: 1/2 yd. assorted beige scraps
Medium print: 1 1/4 yds. assorted pink scraps
Dark print: 5/8 yd. assorted blue scraps
Accent print: 1 1/4 yds. assorted burgundy and brown scraps
Border: 1 7/8 yds.
Backing: 3 yds.
Batting, binding, and thread to finish

Cutting:
A: Cut 8 dark
D: Cut 4 medium
L: Cut 4 light
M: Cut 1 accent

Lattice sections for entire quilt:
A: Cut 152 dark
D: Cut 76 medium
M: Cut 53 accent

Piecing Diagram

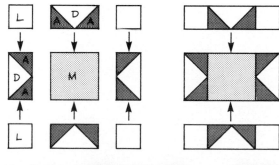

Lattice Section A

Lattice Section B

© Marsha McCloskey, 1985

Dimensions: 52" x 74"
(Color photo, page 16)

Directions:
1. Cut and piece 24 "Road to California" blocks.
2. Cut and piece 18 Lattice sections A.
3. Join 4 "Road to California" blocks with 3 Lattice section A blocks to form a row. Piece together a total of 6 rows.

4. Alternate 7 blocks cut from Template M and 8 Lattice section B units to form a row. Piece 5 of these lattice rows together.

5. Set top together as shown, alternating rows of "Road to California" blocks and lattice rows.
6. Stitch 5 1/2" x 64" rows to each side.
7. Add 5 1/2" x 52" rows to top and bottom of quilt top.
8. Add batting and backing, then quilt or tie.
9. Bind with bias strips.

SISTER'S CHOICE ©

8" block

Dimensions: 42" x 53"
(Color photo, page 72)

Measurements for patterns and borders include 1/4" seam allowance.

Materials: 45" wide yardage
Light print: 3/4 yd. assorted scraps
Dark print: 3/4 yd. assorted scraps
Set piece E: 1/4 yd.
Set piece D: 3/4 yd.
Border: 1 3/8 yds.
Backing: 1 5/8 yds.
Batting, binding, and thread to finish

Cutting:
O: Cut 8 light
    Cut 8 dark
H: Cut 9 dark
    Cut 8 light
Set Piece 5: Cut 20
Set Piece 4: Cut 31

Directions:
1. This quilt has simple borders with straight-sewn corners.
    Cut two 3 1/2" x 47 1/2" strips for length.
    Cut two 3 1/2" x 42 1/2" strips for width.
2. Cut and piece 12 "Sister's Choice" blocks.
3. Set pieced blocks together with Set Piece 4 and 5 as shown.
4. Add 3 1/2" x 47 1/2" straight-sewn borders to sides.
5. Add 3 1/2" x 42 1/2" borders to top and bottom.
6. Add batting and backing, then quilt or tie.
7. Bind with coordinating binding.

Piecing Diagram

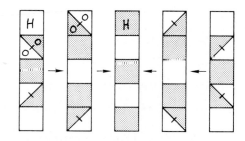

Note: Use the Bias-Strip Piecing technique given on page 147 to quickly piece the triangles.
    Use Template H.

© Marsha McCloskey, 1982

94

WATERWHEEL ©

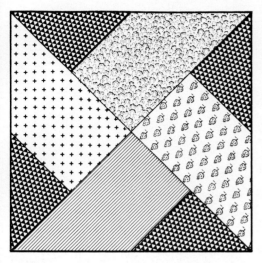

8" block

Dimensions: 49 1/2" x 49 1/2"
(Color photo, page 70)

Measurements for patterns and borders include 1/4" seam allowance.

Materials: 45" wide yardage
  Light print: 1/2 yd. assorted scraps
  Dark print: 1/2 yd. assorted scraps
  Accent print: 3/4 yd. fabric
  Border: 3/8 yd. dark print #1
         1 1/2 yds. dark print #2
  Backing: 1 1/2 yds.
  Batting, binding, and thread to finish

Directions:
1. This quilt has simple borders with straight-sewn corners.
   Cut two 5" x 40 1/2" strips from dark print #1.
   Cut two 5" x 49 1/2" strips from dark print #2.
2. Cut and piece 25 "Waterwheel" blocks.
3. Set pieced blocks together as shown.
4. Add 5" x 40 1/2" strips to sides.
5. Stitch 5" x 49 1/2" strips to top and bottom.
6. Add batting and backing, then quilt or tie.
7. Bind with coordinated binding.

Cutting:
  D: Cut 4 accent
  G: Cut 2 light
      Cut 2 dark

Piecing Diagram

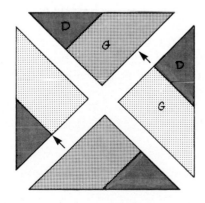 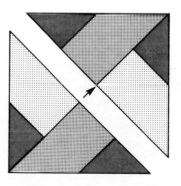

95

WHIRLYGIG©

8" block

Measurements for patterns and borders include 1/4" seam allowance.

Materials: 45" wide yardage

Light print: 1 yd. assorted scraps
Medium print: 1/2 yd. assorted scraps
Dark print: 1 yd. assorted scraps
Border: 3/8 yd. dark print #1
       5/8 yd. dark print #2
Backing: 3 1/8 yds.
Batting, binding, and thread to finish

Cutting:

B: Cut 4 light
D: Cut 4 dark
      Cut 4 medium

Piecing Diagram

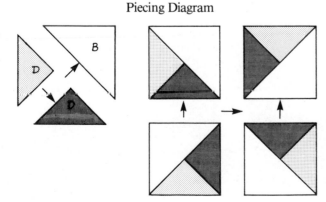

Dimensions: 52 1/2" x 52 1/2"
  (Color photo, page 65)

Directions:

1. This quilt has 2 simple straight-sewn borders and an accent corner block.
   Cut two 2 1/2" x 40 1/2" strips from dark print #1.
   Cut two 2 1/2" x 44 1/2" strips from dark print #1.
   Cut four 4 1/2" x 44 1/2" strips from dark print #2.
2. Cut and piece 25 "Whirlygig" blocks.
3. Set pieced blocks together as shown.
4. Add 2 1/2" x 40 1/2" borders to sides.
5. Stitch 2 1/2" x 44 1/2" borders to top and bottom.
6. Piece 4 corner segments. Stitch two segments to the ends of two 4 1/2" x 44 1/2" borders.
7. Add 4 1/2" x 44 1/2" borders to sides.
8. Stitch remaining border with corner segments attached to top and bottom.
9. Add batting and backing, then quilt or tie.
10. Bind with coordinated binding.

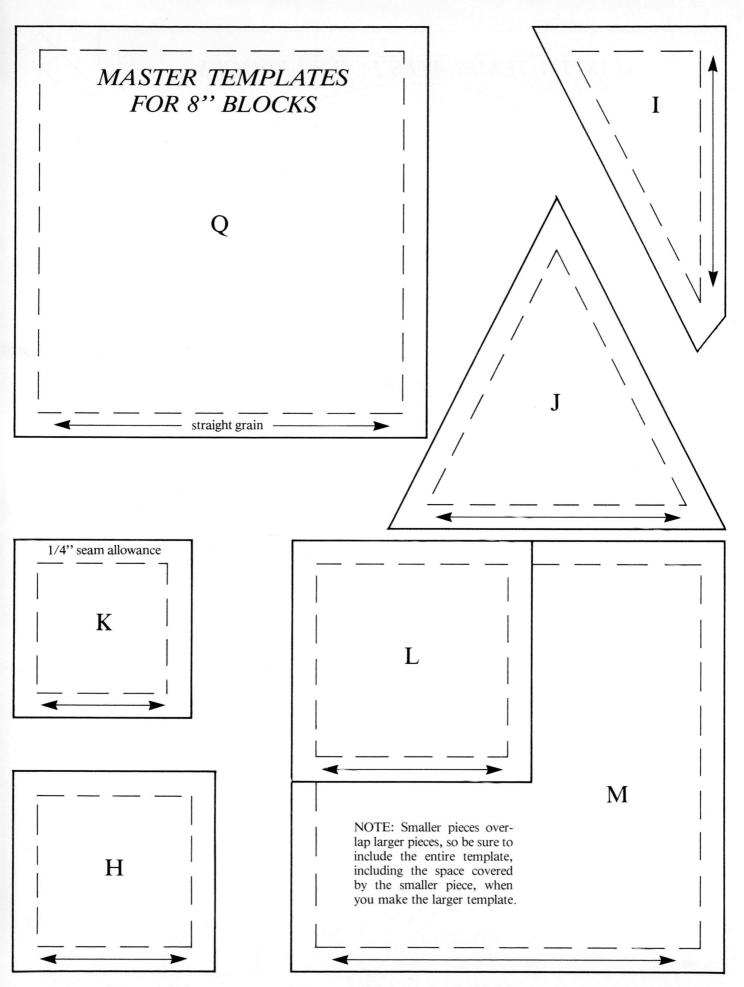

MASTER TEMPLATES
FOR 8" BLOCKS

Q

straight grain

I

J

1/4" seam allowance

K

L

H

M

NOTE: Smaller pieces overlap larger pieces, so be sure to
include the entire template,
including the space covered
by the smaller piece, when
you make the larger template.

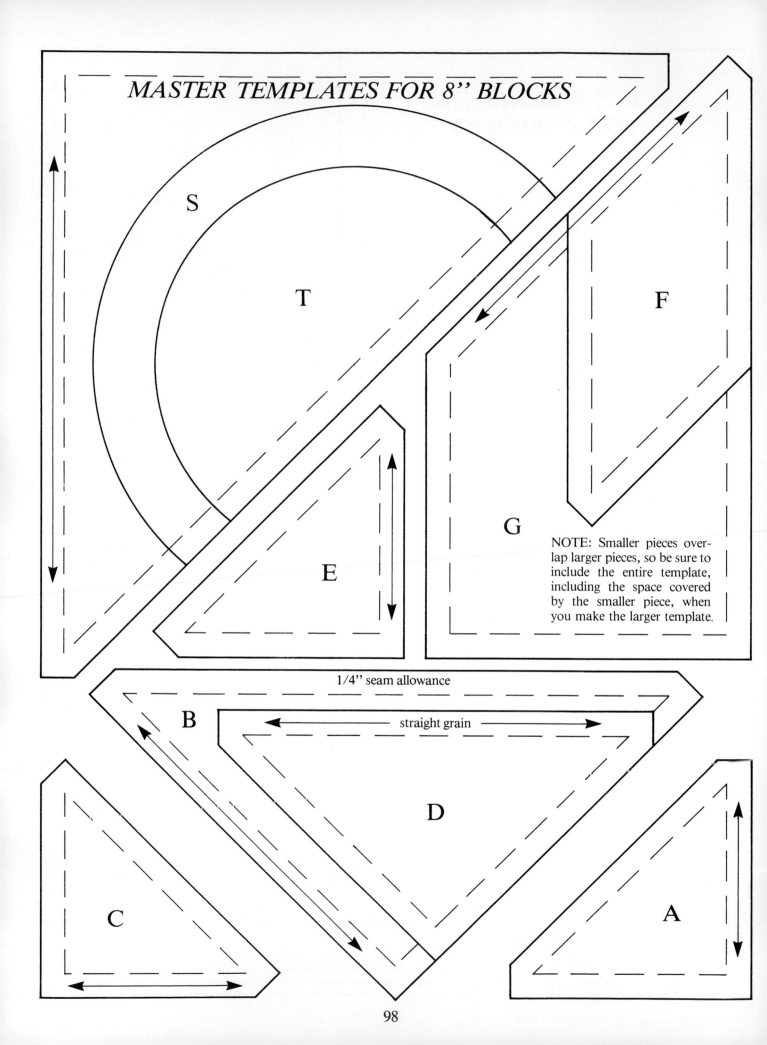

MASTER TEMPLATES FOR 8" BLOCKS

S

T

F

E

G

NOTE: Smaller pieces overlap larger pieces, so be sure to include the entire template, including the space covered by the smaller piece, when you make the larger template.

1/4" seam allowance

B

straight grain

D

C

A

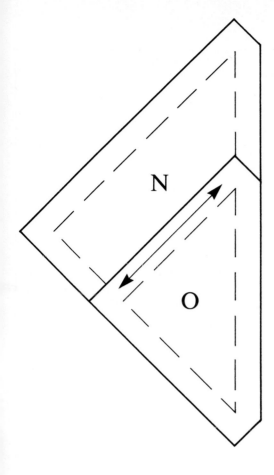

N

O

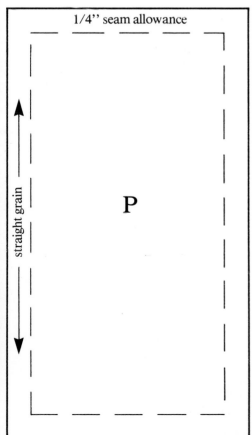

1/4" seam allowance

straight grain

P

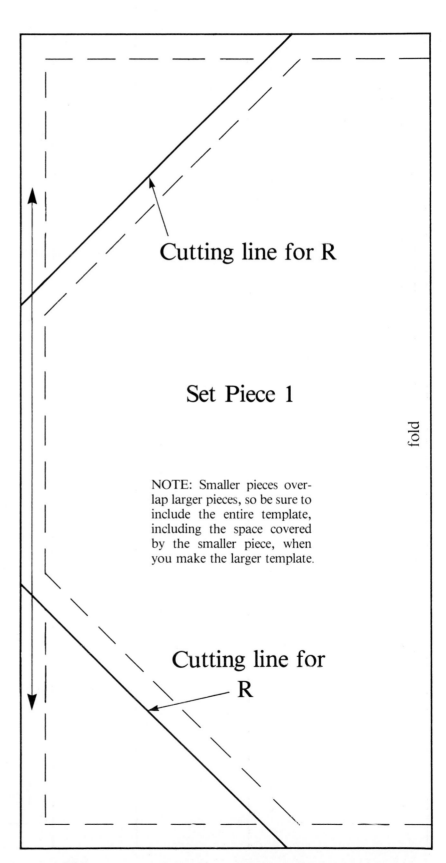

Cutting line for R

Set Piece 1

fold

NOTE: Smaller pieces overlap larger pieces, so be sure to
include the entire template,
including the space covered
by the smaller piece, when
you make the larger template.

Cutting line for
R

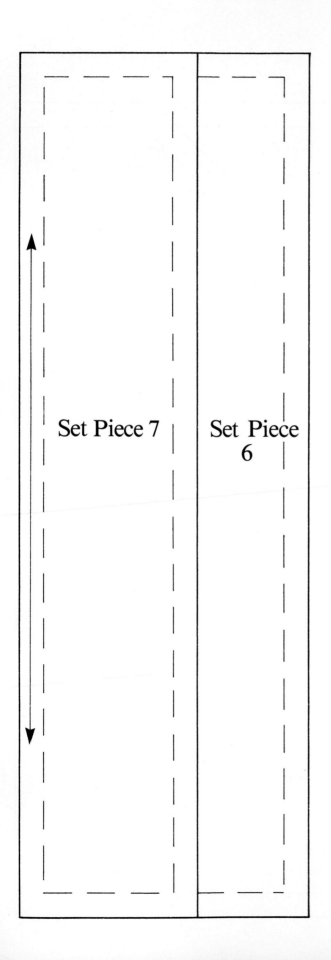

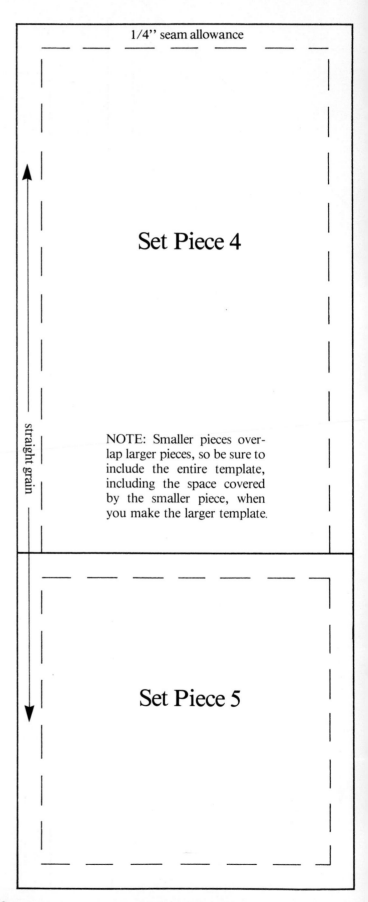

1/4" seam allowance

Set Piece 4

straight grain

NOTE: Smaller pieces overlap larger pieces, so be sure to
include the entire template,
including the space covered
by the smaller piece, when
you make the larger template.

Set Piece 5

Set Piece 7

Set Piece 6

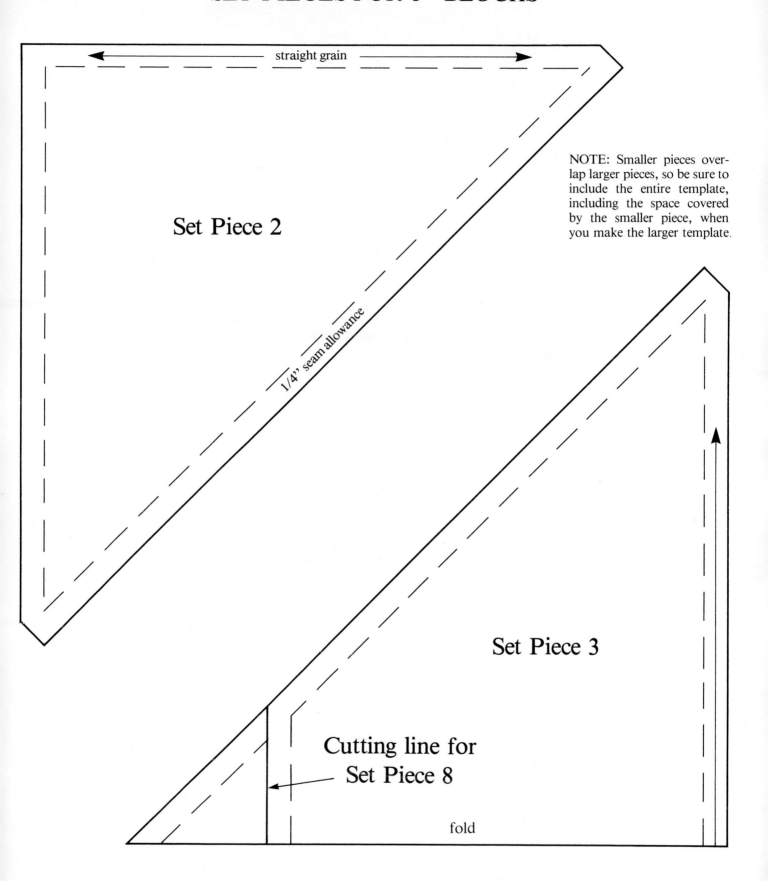

straight grain

Set Piece 2

1/4" seam allowance

NOTE: Smaller pieces over-lap larger pieces, so be sure to include the entire template, including the space covered by the smaller piece, when you make the larger template.

Set Piece 3

Cutting line for
Set Piece 8

fold

TWELVE-INCH QUILT BLOCKS AND MASTER QUILT PLANS

There are patterns for sixteen 12″ quilt blocks in this section of the book: Bear's Paw, Birds in the Air, Caesar's Crown, Cherry Basket, Cut Glass Dish, Dutchman's Puzzle, Feathered World Without End, Goose in the Pond, Grandmother's Fan, Homespun Houses, Hosannah, Jacob's Ladder, Lady of the Lake, Ocean Waves, Puss in a Corner, Tree of Life, and Weathervane. Master Quilt Plans are provided at the beginning of this section which can be used to accommodate any 12″ block.

Templates

To make each unit block, you will need a set of pattern pieces or templates. Carefully trace the templates from the book onto graph paper or tracing paper. Trace accurately and transfer to the paper all information printed on the templates in the book.

Each template for the unit blocks is labeled with a number, the design name, the finished block size, and the number to cut for one block. A notation such as "Cut 4 + 4" indicates the same template is used for two colors in the design. An "R" in a cutting notation means "reverse". The pieces are mirror images: cut the first number of pieces with the template face up and then flip it over face down to cut the remainder.

Templates have seam lines (broken lines) as well as cutting lines (solid lines). Grainlines are for the lengthwise or crosswise grain and are shown with an arrow on each piece. Fold lines indicate where half templates are given due to space limitations. Complete the other half of the pattern when you make larger templates. Consult the Glossary of Techniques on page 145-150 for complete directions on quiltmaking techniques.

Solid Set

Some blocks look best when set together side by side, such as the Bear's Paw on page 108, Feathered World Without End, on page 114, and Puss in A Corner on page 123. The secondary design at the corners where the blocks meet would be lost in any other set.

Bear's Paw Blocks

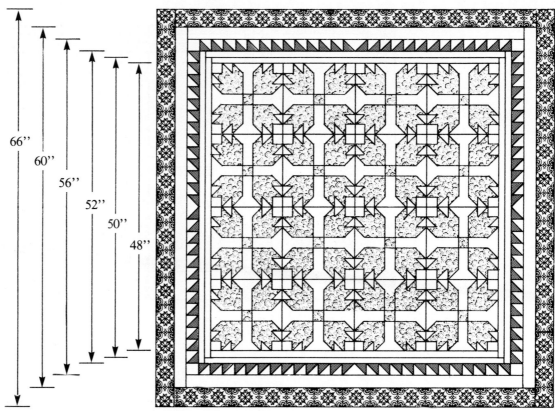

Puss in A Corner Blocks

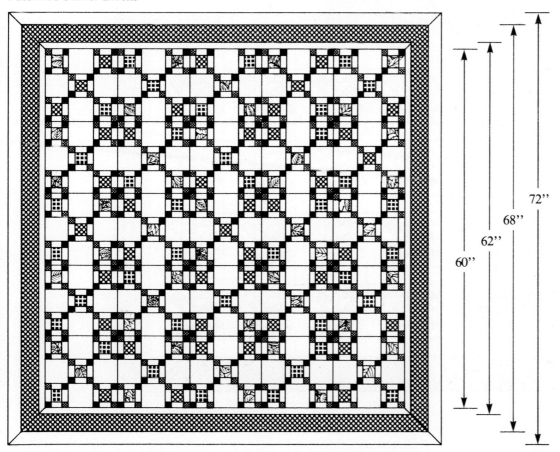

Lattice Sets

Some quilt blocks look best when separated by lattice strips and squares. These are called set pieces and can be plain or pieced. Lattice strips, both pieced and plain can also be used with diagonally set blocks.

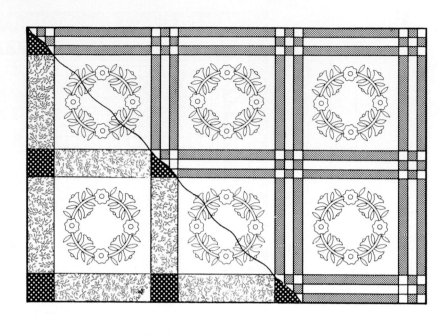

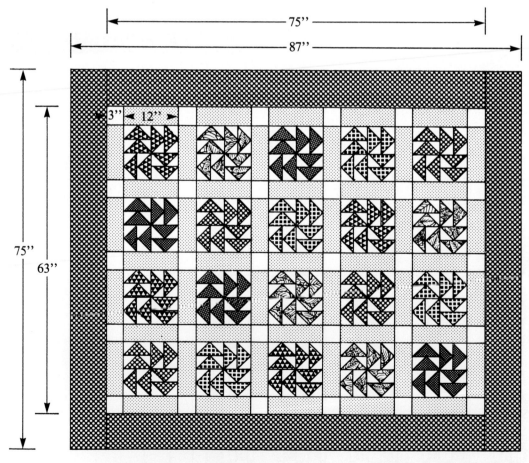

Dutchman's Puzzle Blocks

Diagonal Sets

The diagonal set is the most appropriate for several directional blocks such as Cherry Basket or Tree of Life. It can add additional interest to blocks like Grandmother's Fan and Ocean Waves. Pieced blocks may be alternated with plain blocks in a diagonal set to create areas where elaborate quilting designs may be used.

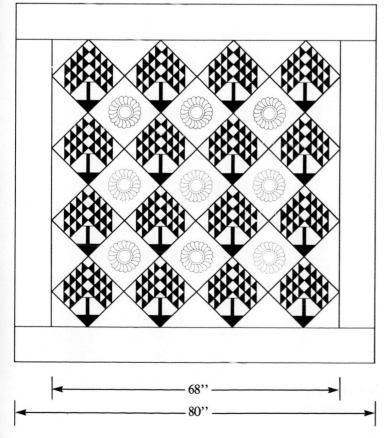

Tree of Life with Feathered Quilting

68"

80"

Ocean Waves

85"

67"

Dimensions for Cutting Set Pieces:
  Alternate Block: 12 1/2" x 12 1/2"
  Side Triangles: 12 1/2" x 12 1/2" x 17 5/8"
  Corner Triangles: 9" x 9" x 12 3/4"

A 12" block set diagonally measures 16.97"

16.97"

105

Barnraising Set

The word "Barnraising"* is used to describe a set that radiates concentrically from the center of a quilt. Log Cabin blocks are commonly arranged this way, with their dark and light sides forming an overall pattern. The Barnraising set can also be achieved using the Homespun House or Cut Glass Dish with pieced triangle blocks.

Homespun House 11" blocks set with pieced triangle blocks

* This type of set is referred to as Barnraising because it reminded early quilters of the arrangement of logs and boards used when they gathered to help a neighbor erect a barn.

Fabric Requirements

To get a "ball park" figure or rough estimate of the fabric needed for a quilt, first figure the yardage for the quilt backing. For example, a finished quilt 80" x 104" would require six yards of fabric for the backing: two three-yard lengths (108") of 45"-wide fabric, seamed down the middle to get the 80" width. Then multiply the amount of fabric needed for the backing (six yards in this case) by 1.5.

6 yards x 1.5 = 9 yards

Nine yards is a conservative rough estimate of fabric needed for the quilt top. Use it for reference. The amount of fabric you actually need will probably be a bit more. Figure the yardage as outlined below, then look at the total. Is it close to your rough estimate? If your calculations total 3 1/2 yards (nowhere near nine yards), you'll know there is something wrong. Likewise, a 40 yard total is unreasonable. Ten yards or 11 1/2 yards, however, is in the "ball park."

To figure specific yardage requirements, you will need a quilt plan. This is generally a scale drawing on graph paper that shows unit block design and size; type of set and number of set pieces; and indicates border treatment and dimensions. Sample quilt plans are given on pages 103-106.

Base yardage requirements on a good quilt plan and follow these steps.

1. Identify and make templates for all the shapes in the quilt design, i.e., pieces in the patterned blocks and the set pieces (lattices or alternate blocks). You don't have to make templates for larger border pieces; knowing their dimensions is enough.

2. For each template, write the number of pieces to be cut from each fabric in your design.

3. Armed with shapes, sizes and numbers, proceed to figure out how many of each template will fit on the usable width of the fabric. With fabric that is 45" on the bolt, you can really count on a usable width of only 42". Selvages should be cut off and you must allow for some shrinkage. For example, twelve 8 1/2" squares are needed as set pieces in the quilt plan. Divide 42" by 8.5" and find that four complete squares can be cut from the width of the fabric. Each set of four squares requires 8.5 linear inches of fabric. To get 12 squares, 3 x 8.5" or 25.5 linear inches of fabric are needed. This is nearly 3/4 yard (27"), but to buy only 3/4 yard would be cutting it pretty close. I would go on to the next highest eighth of a yard and buy 7/8 yard. It is a good idea to buy at least four extra inches of a fabric to allow for shrinkage, straightening and cutting mistakes.

Complete this process for each shape and fabric in the quilt plan. Total the amounts and compare with your ball park figure. If it seems reasonable, you are ready to buy.

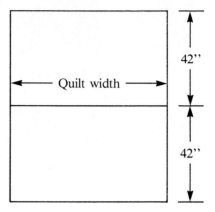

Seam together fabric for quilt backing.

BEAR'S PAW

12" block
(Color photo, page 18)

Piecing Diagram

Make 4

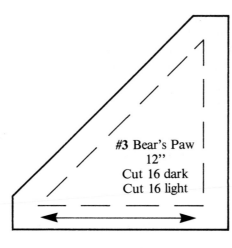
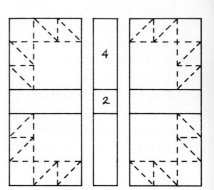

#2 Bear's Paw
12"
Cut 4 light
Cut 1 dark

#3 Bear's Paw
12"
Cut 16 dark
Cut 16 light

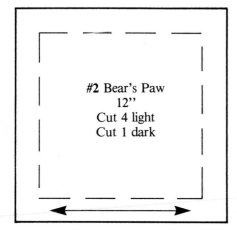

1/4" seam allowance

#4 Bear's Paw
12"
Cut 4 light

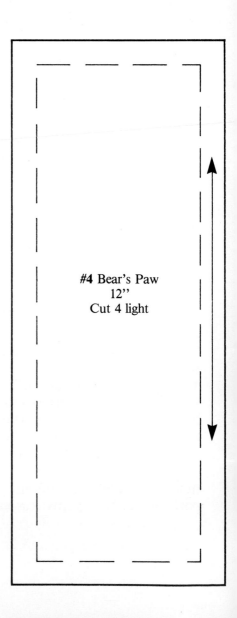

#1 Bear's Paw
12"
Cut 4 dark

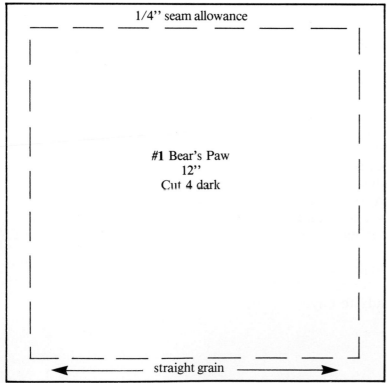

straight grain

BIRDS IN THE AIR

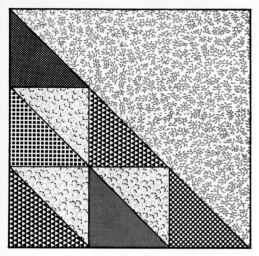

12" block
(Color photo, page 37 and 67)

Piecing Diagram

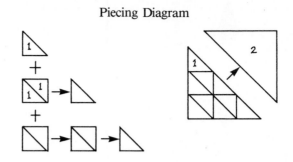

Use the Bias-Strip Piecing technique given on page 147 to quickly piece the triangles.

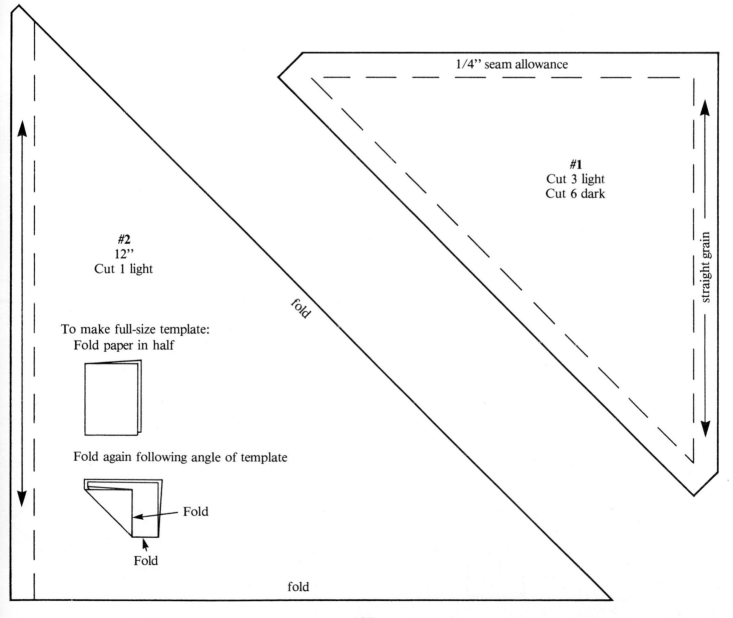

1/4" seam allowance

#1
Cut 3 light
Cut 6 dark

straight grain

#2
12"
Cut 1 light

To make full-size template:
Fold paper in half

Fold again following angle of template

Fold

Fold

fold

fold

109

CAESAR'S CROWN

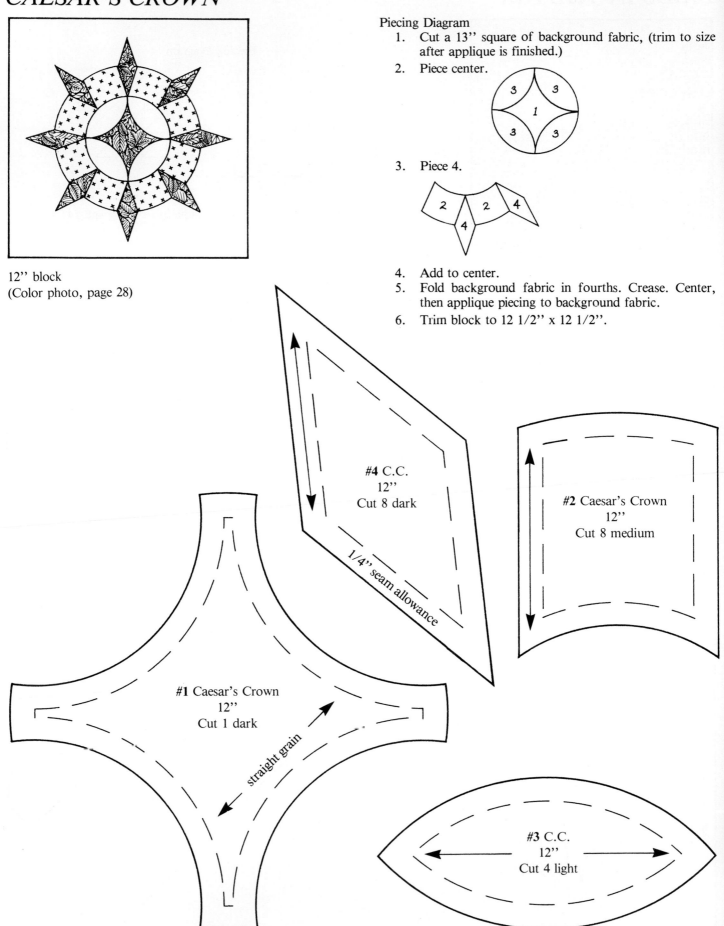

12" block
(Color photo, page 28)

Piecing Diagram
1. Cut a 13" square of background fabric, (trim to size after applique is finished.)
2. Piece center.
3. Piece 4.
4. Add to center.
5. Fold background fabric in fourths. Crease. Center, then applique piecing to background fabric.
6. Trim block to 12 1/2" x 12 1/2".

#4 C.C.
12"
Cut 8 dark

1/4" seam allowance

#2 Caesar's Crown
12"
Cut 8 medium

#1 Caesar's Crown
12"
Cut 1 dark

straight grain

#3 C.C.
12"
Cut 4 light

CHERRY BASKET

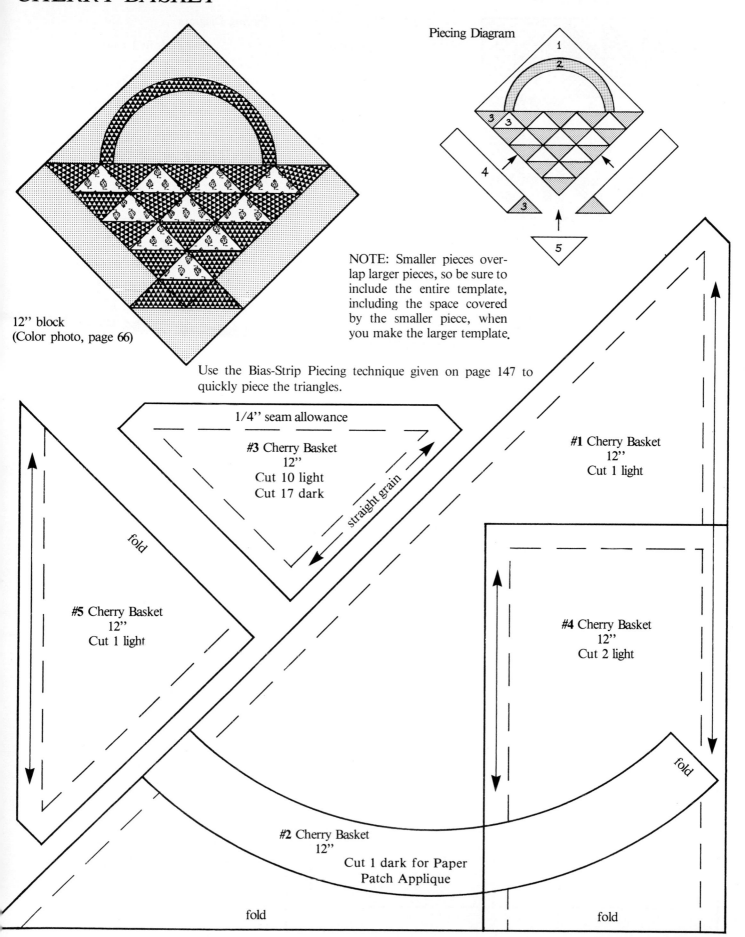

Piecing Diagram

12" block
(Color photo, page 66)

NOTE: Smaller pieces overlap larger pieces, so be sure to include the entire template, including the space covered by the smaller piece, when you make the larger template.

Use the Bias-Strip Piecing technique given on page 147 to quickly piece the triangles.

1/4" seam allowance

#3 Cherry Basket
12"
Cut 10 light
Cut 17 dark

straight grain

#1 Cherry Basket
12"
Cut 1 light

fold

#5 Cherry Basket
12"
Cut 1 light

#4 Cherry Basket
12"
Cut 2 light

fold

#2 Cherry Basket
12"
Cut 1 dark for Paper
Patch Applique

fold

fold

fold

111

CUT GLASS DISH

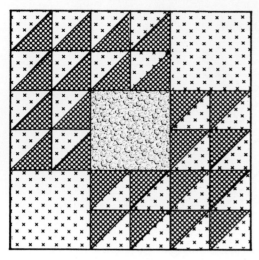

12" block
(Color photo, page 33)

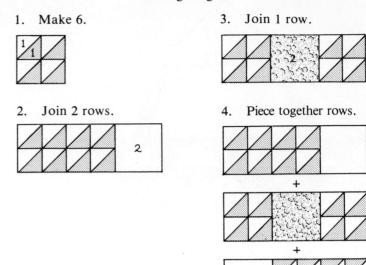

1. Make 6.

3. Join 1 row.

2. Join 2 rows.

4. Piece together rows.

Use the Bias-Strip Piecing technique given on page 147 to quickly piece the triangles.

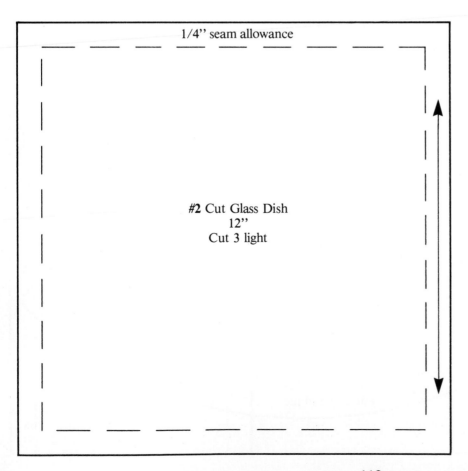

1/4" seam allowance

#2 Cut Glass Dish
12"
Cut 3 light

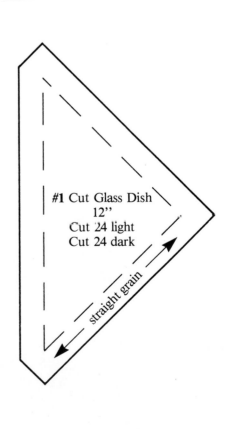

#1 Cut Glass Dish
12"
Cut 24 light
Cut 24 dark

straight grain

DUTCHMAN'S PUZZLE

12" block
(Color photo, page 40)

Piecing Diagram

1. Make 8.

2. Piece 2 rows.

3. Join rows.

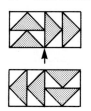

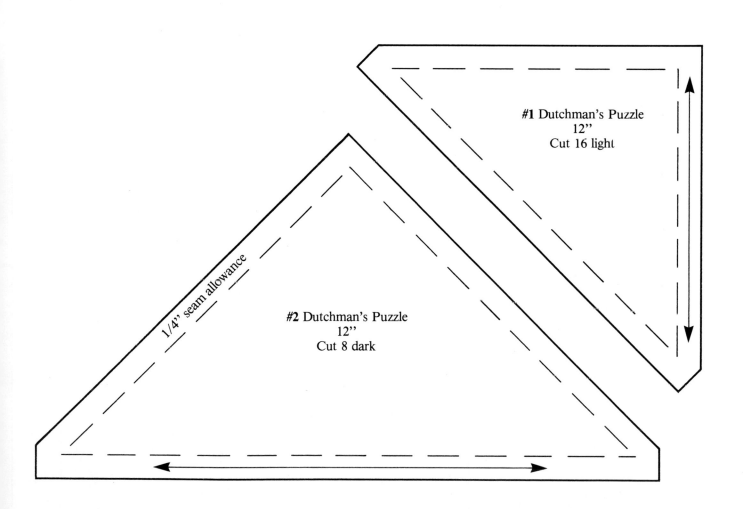

1/4" seam allowance

#2 Dutchman's Puzzle
12"
Cut 8 dark

#1 Dutchman's Puzzle
12"
Cut 16 light

FEATHERED WORLD WITHOUT END©

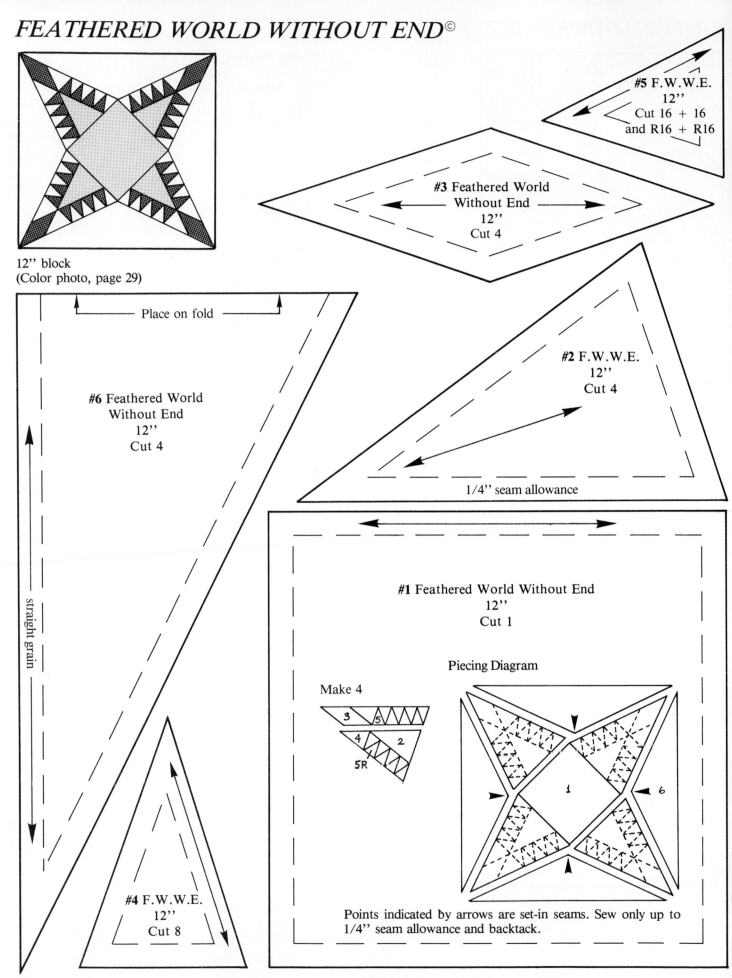

12" block
(Color photo, page 29)

#5 F.W.W.E.
12"
Cut 16 + 16
and R16 + R16

#3 Feathered World
Without End
12"
Cut 4

Place on fold

#6 Feathered World
Without End
12"
Cut 4

#2 F.W.W.E.
12"
Cut 4

1/4" seam allowance

straight grain

#1 Feathered World Without End
12"
Cut 1

Piecing Diagram

Make 4

3 5
4 2
5R

1 6

#4 F.W.W.E.
12"
Cut 8

Points indicated by arrows are set-in seams. Sew only up to
1/4" seam allowance and backtack.

GOOSE IN THE POND©

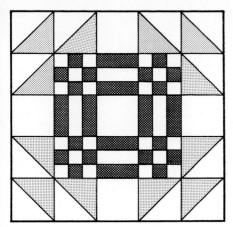

12'' block
(Color photo, page 33)

Piecing Diagram

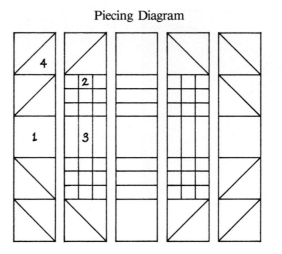

Although templates for each piece are given here, this block
could easily be adapted to strip piecing techniques.

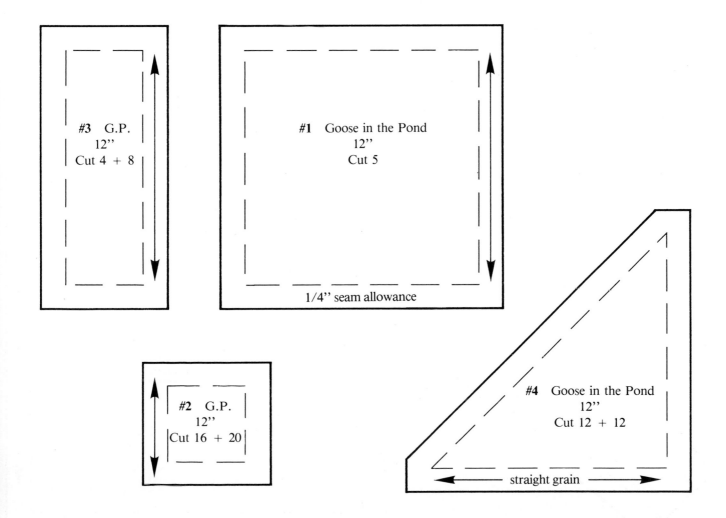

#3 G.P.
12''
Cut 4 + 8

#1 Goose in the Pond
12''
Cut 5

1/4'' seam allowance

#2 G.P.
12''
Cut 16 + 20

#4 Goose in the Pond
12''
Cut 12 + 12

straight grain

115

GRANDMOTHER'S FAN

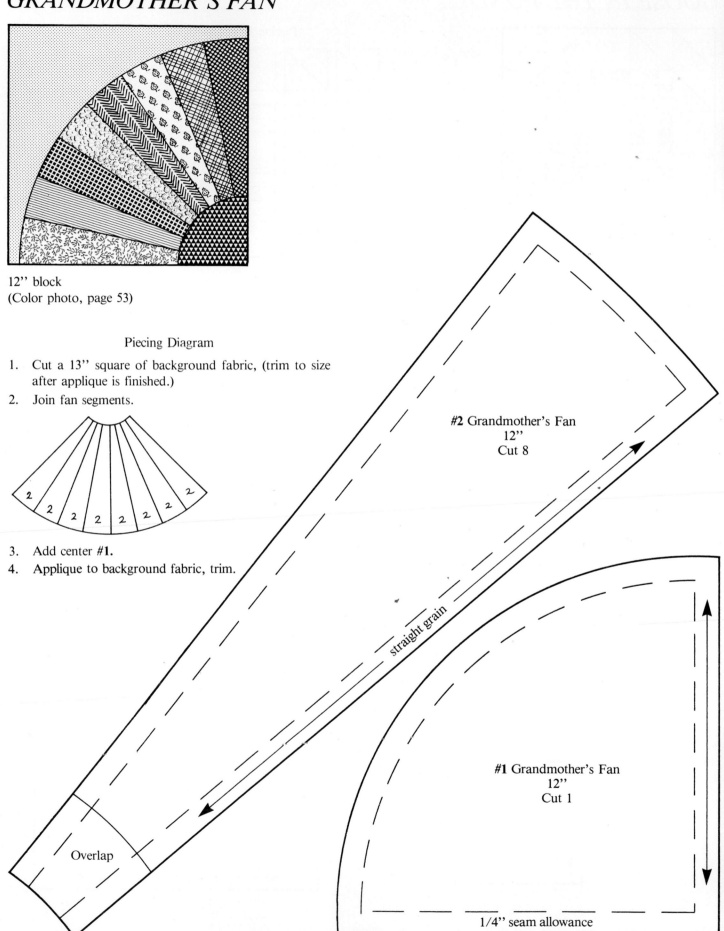

12" block
(Color photo, page 53)

Piecing Diagram

1. Cut a 13" square of background fabric, (trim to size after applique is finished.)
2. Join fan segments.

3. Add center **#1.**
4. Applique to background fabric, trim.

#2 Grandmother's Fan
12"
Cut 8

straight grain

Overlap

#1 Grandmother's Fan
12"
Cut 1

1/4" seam allowance

HOMESPUN HOUSES

11" block
(Color photo, page 64)

NOTE: Add a 1/2" border of background fabric to all four sides of block to make a 12" block that can be used in the Master Quilt Plans found on pages 103-105.

Piecing Diagram

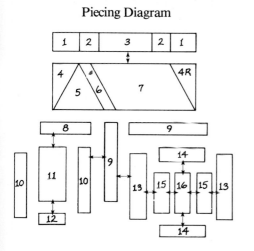

NOTE: Smaller pieces overlap larger pieces, so be sure to include the entire template, including the space covered by the smaller piece, when you make the larger template.

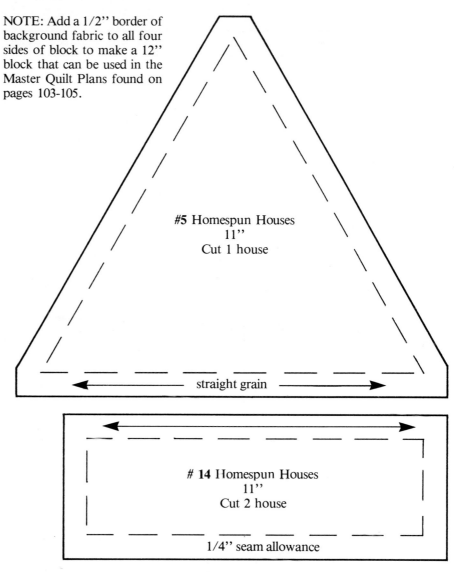

#5 Homespun Houses
11"
Cut 1 house

straight grain

 # 14 Homespun Houses
11"
Cut 2 house

1/4" seam allowance

#15 Homespun Houses
11"
Cut 2 background

#13 Homespun Houses
11"
Cut 2 house

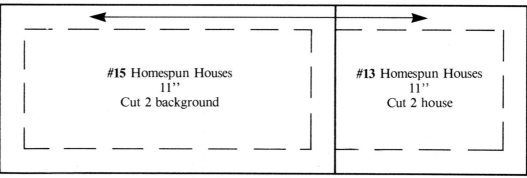

#12 Homespun Houses
11"
Cut 1 house

#16
H.H.
Cut 1
house

#8
H.H.
Cut 1
house

#10
H.H.
Cut 2
house

#9
H.H.
Cut 2
background

HOMESPUN HOUSES

11'' block

NOTE: Smaller pieces overlap larger pieces, so be sure to include the entire template, including the space covered by the smaller piece, when you make the larger template.

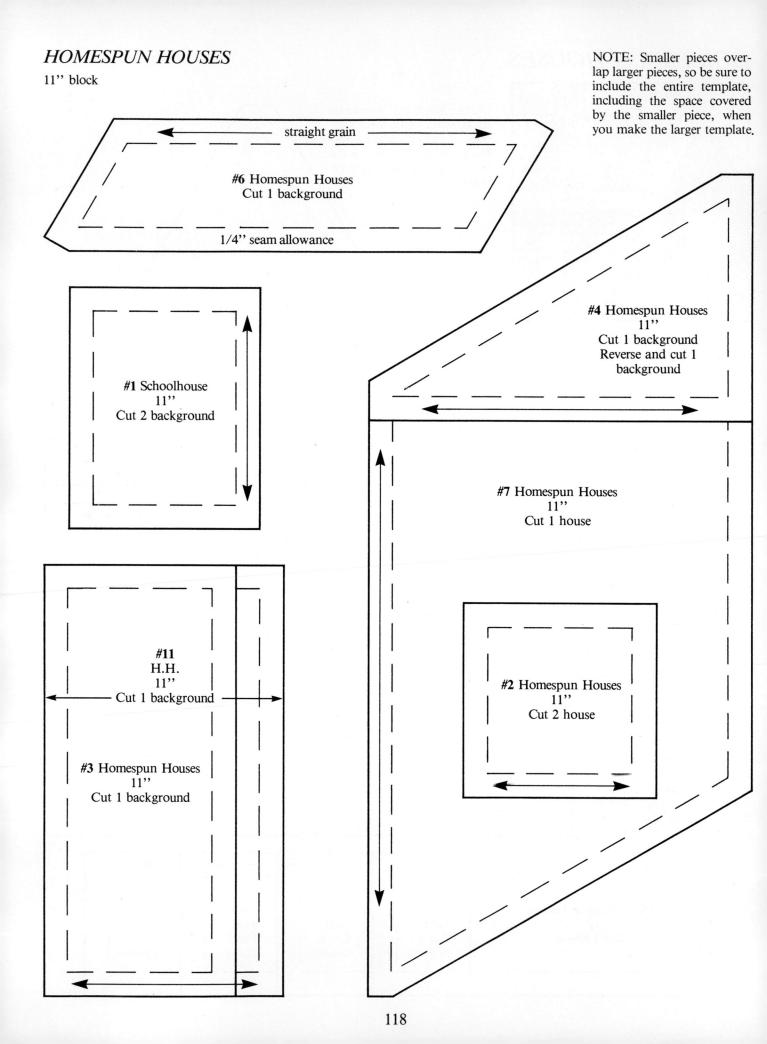

straight grain

#6 Homespun Houses
Cut 1 background

1/4'' seam allowance

#1 Schoolhouse
11''
Cut 2 background

#4 Homespun Houses
11''
Cut 1 background
Reverse and cut 1
background

#7 Homespun Houses
11''
Cut 1 house

#11
H.H.
11''
Cut 1 background

#3 Homespun Houses
11''
Cut 1 background

#2 Homespun Houses
11''
Cut 2 house

HOSANNAH (PALM LEAF)

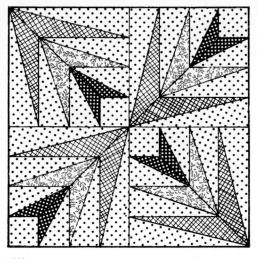

12"
(Color photo, page 28)

NOTE: Smaller pieces overlap larger pieces, so be sure to
include the entire template,
including the space covered
by the smaller piece, when
you make the larger template.

Piecing Diagram

1. Make 4 each.

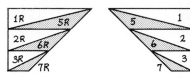

2. Piece together.

3. Join segments together.

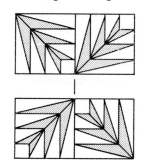

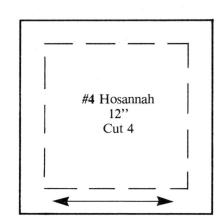

#4 Hosannah
12"
Cut 4

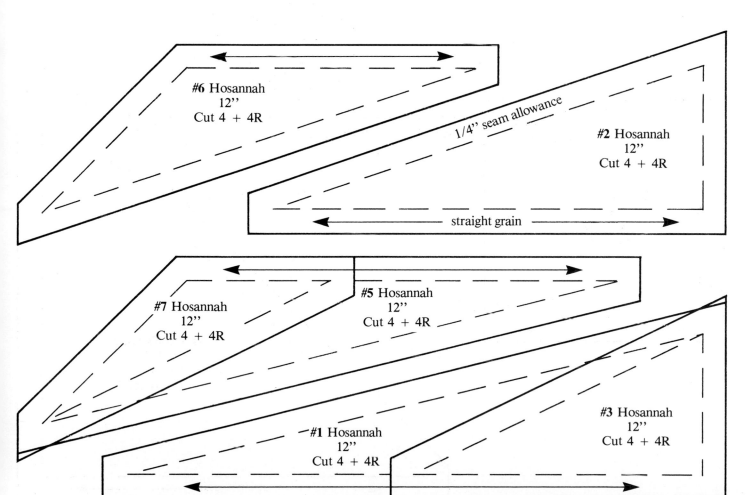

#6 Hosannah
12"
Cut 4 + 4R

1/4" seam allowance

#2 Hosannah
12"
Cut 4 + 4R

straight grain

#7 Hosannah
12"
Cut 4 + 4R

#5 Hosannah
12"
Cut 4 + 4R

#1 Hosannah
12"
Cut 4 + 4R

#3 Hosannah
12"
Cut 4 + 4R

JACOB'S LADDER

12" block
(Color photo, page 27)

Piecing Diagram

1. Make 5.

2. Make 4.

3. Join in rows.

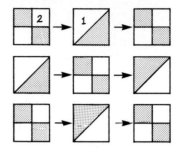

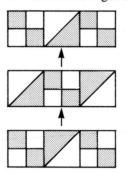

4. Join rows together.

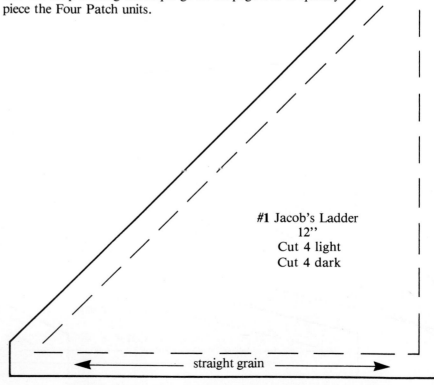

Use the Strip Piecing technique given on page 146 to quickly piece the Four Patch units.

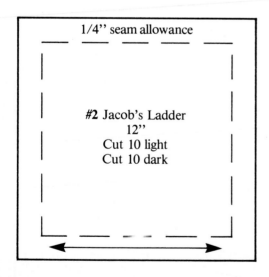

1/4" seam allowance

#2 Jacob's Ladder
12"
Cut 10 light
Cut 10 dark

#1 Jacob's Ladder
12"
Cut 4 light
Cut 4 dark

straight grain

120

LADY OF THE LAKE

12" block
(Color photo, page 22)

Piecing Diagram

1. Make 16.

2. Join

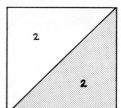

3. Add triangle segments.

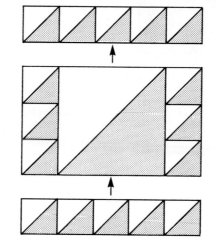

Use the Bias-Strip Piecing technique given on page 147 to quickly piece the triangles.

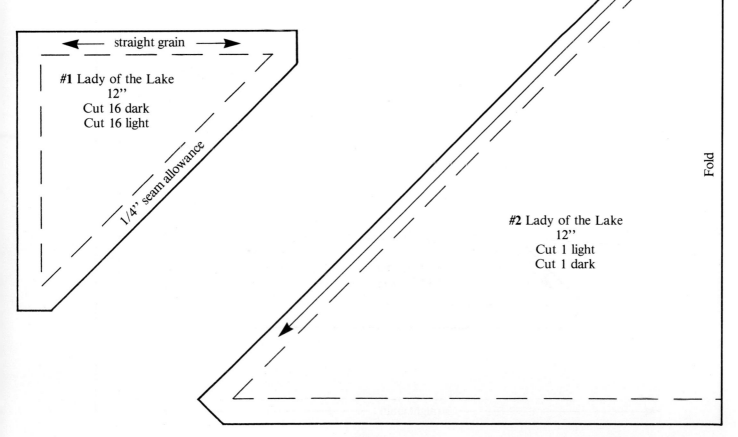

straight grain

#1 Lady of the Lake
12"
Cut 16 dark
Cut 16 light

1/4" seam allowance

#2 Lady of the Lake
12"
Cut 1 light
Cut 1 dark

Fold

OCEAN WAVES

12" block
(Color photo, pages 21 and 67)

Piecing Diagram

1. Piece 4.

2. Add to sides.

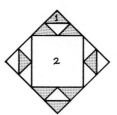

3. Piece 4.

4. Add to corners.

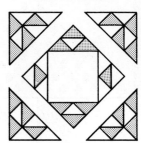

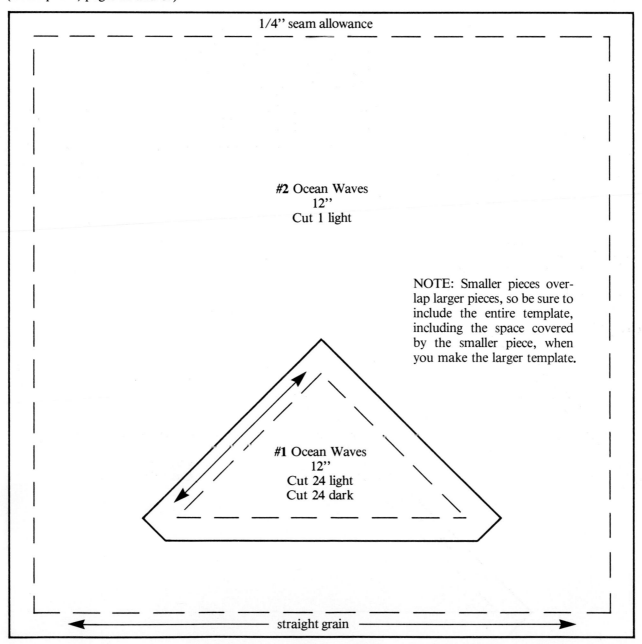

1/4" seam allowance

#2 Ocean Waves
12"
Cut 1 light

NOTE: Smaller pieces overlap larger pieces, so be sure to include the entire template, including the space covered by the smaller piece, when you make the larger template.

#1 Ocean Waves
12"
Cut 24 light
Cut 24 dark

straight grain

PUSS IN A CORNER

12" block
(Color photo, page 37)

(Color photo, page 37)

Piecing Diagram

1. Piece 5.

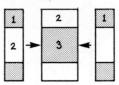
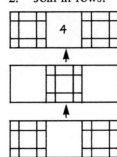

2. Join in rows.

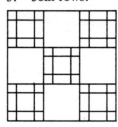

3. Join rows.

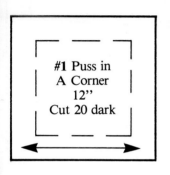

#1 Puss in
A Corner
12"
Cut 20 dark

#2 Puss in A Corner
12"
Cut 20 light

#3 Puss in A Corner
12"
Cut 5 dark

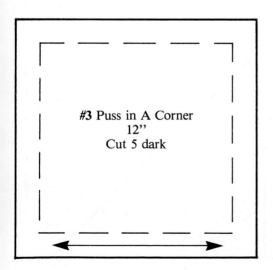

1/4" seam allowance

#4 Puss in A Corner
12"
Cut 4 light

straight grain

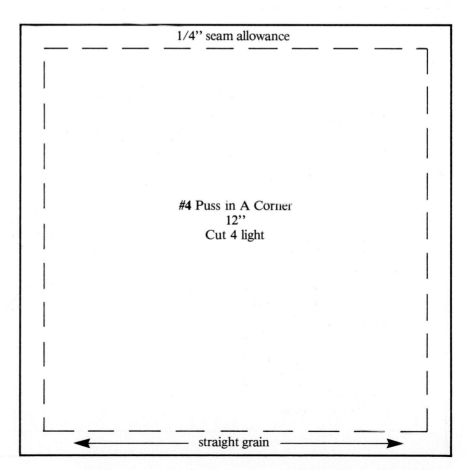

123

TREE OF LIFE©

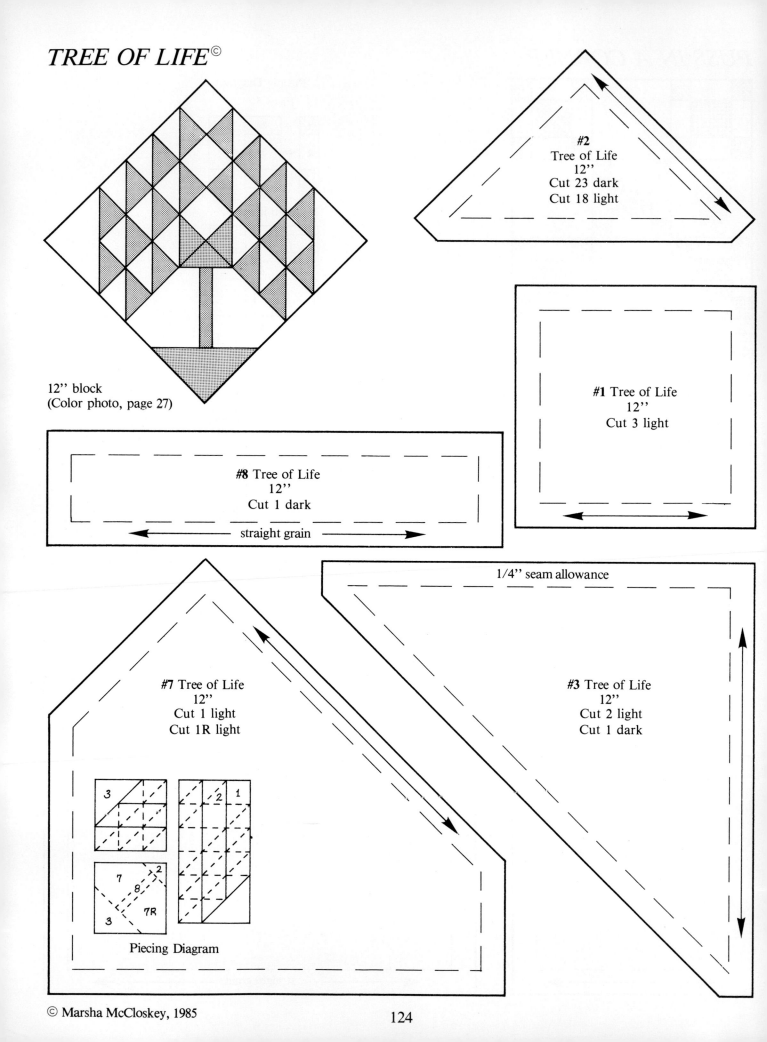

12" block
(Color photo, page 27)

#2
Tree of Life
12"
Cut 23 dark
Cut 18 light

#1 Tree of Life
12"
Cut 3 light

#8 Tree of Life
12"
Cut 1 dark

straight grain

1/4" seam allowance

#7 Tree of Life
12"
Cut 1 light
Cut 1R light

#3 Tree of Life
12"
Cut 2 light
Cut 1 dark

Piecing Diagram

WEATHERVANE

12" block
(Color photo, page 36)

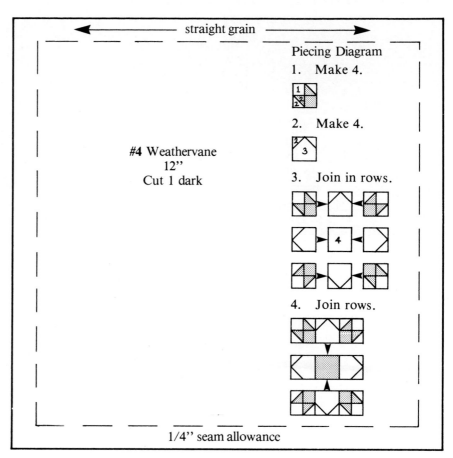

straight grain

Piecing Diagram

1. Make 4.

2. Make 4.

#4 Weathervane
12"
Cut 1 dark

3. Join in rows.

4. Join rows.

1/4" seam allowance

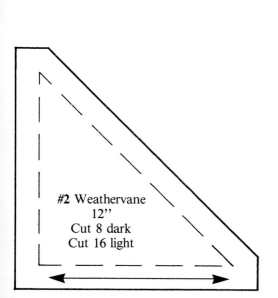

#2 Weathervane
12"
Cut 8 dark
Cut 16 light

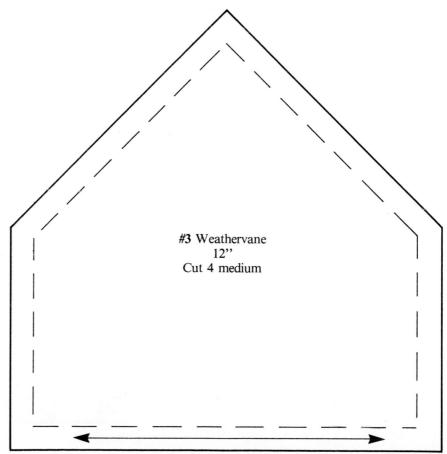

#3 Weathervane
12"
Cut 4 medium

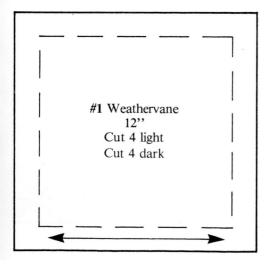

#1 Weathervane
12"
Cut 4 light
Cut 4 dark

LOG CABIN QUILT BLOCKS

10" Log Cabin block

(Color photos, pages 18, 31, and 50)

Courthouse Steps variation

The Log Cabin block with its simple charm is one of the oldest types of patchwork, dating back to the mid 1800s. There are many variations and setting arrangements of the Log Cabin block. Changing the color, size, and sequence of fabric will produce varied Log Cabin blocks. Courthouse Steps is a common variation of the Log Cabin block.

The Log Cabin block is constructed of strips which are pieced around a center square. Traditionally the Log Cabin block is diagonally divided into lights and darks, or into two contrasting colors. The Log Cabin lends itself to a scrap quilt because of the narrow strips of fabric required.

There are several popular setting arrangements for the Log Cabin blocks: Barnraising, Straight Furrows, Sunshine and Shadows, and Pinwheel. The same Log Cabin block is used in all of these sets, only the placement of the blocks varies. Log Cabin blocks are set together without lattice to form an overall design. Construct the number of blocks needed to achieve finished size. Borders may be added.

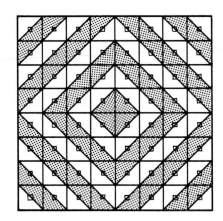

Barnraising

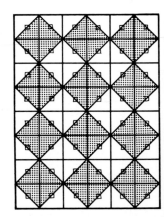

Sunshine and Shadows

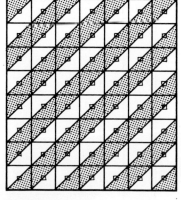

Straight Furrows

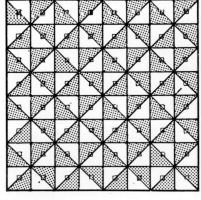

Pinwheel

126

LOG CABIN

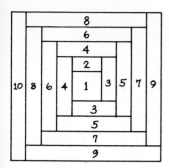

Piecing Diagram

Join pieces 1 and 2, add piece 3, etc.

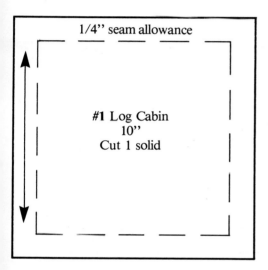

1/4" seam allowance

#1 Log Cabin
10"
Cut 1 solid

NOTE: Smaller pieces overlap larger pieces, so be sure to
include the entire template,
including the space covered
by the smaller piece, when
you make the larger template.

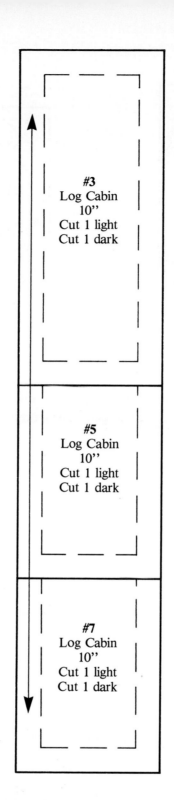

#3
Log Cabin
10"
Cut 1 light
Cut 1 dark

#5
Log Cabin
10"
Cut 1 light
Cut 1 dark

#7
Log Cabin
10"
Cut 1 light
Cut 1 dark

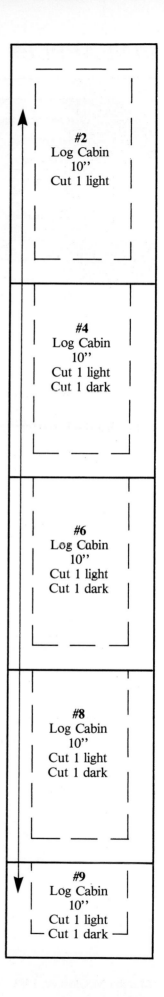

#2
Log Cabin
10"
Cut 1 light

#4
Log Cabin
10"
Cut 1 light
Cut 1 dark

#6
Log Cabin
10"
Cut 1 light
Cut 1 dark

#8
Log Cabin
10"
Cut 1 light
Cut 1 dark

#9
Log Cabin
10"
Cut 1 light
Cut 1 dark

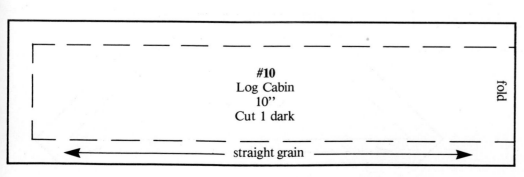

#10
Log Cabin
10"
Cut 1 dark

fold

← straight grain →

PINEAPPLE©

12" block
(Color photo, page 57)

Piecing Diagram

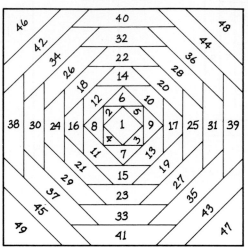

Piecing Diagram

A Log Cabin variation, the Pineapple has an accent color for the center. The rest of the pieces are arranged in a strong light-and-dark pattern consisting of many fabrics.

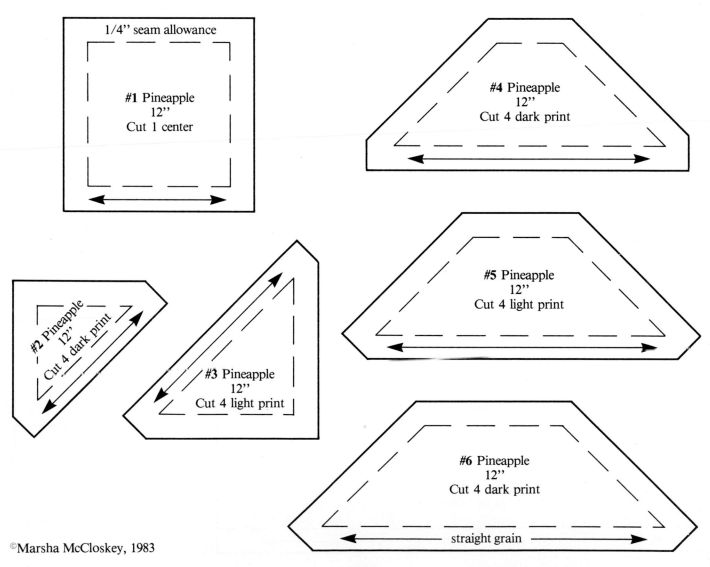

1/4" seam allowance

#1 Pineapple
12"
Cut 1 center

#2 Pineapple
12"
Cut 4 dark print

#3 Pineapple
12"
Cut 4 light print

#4 Pineapple
12"
Cut 4 dark print

#5 Pineapple
12"
Cut 4 light print

#6 Pineapple
12"
Cut 4 dark print

straight grain

©Marsha McCloskey, 1983

128

PINEAPPLE

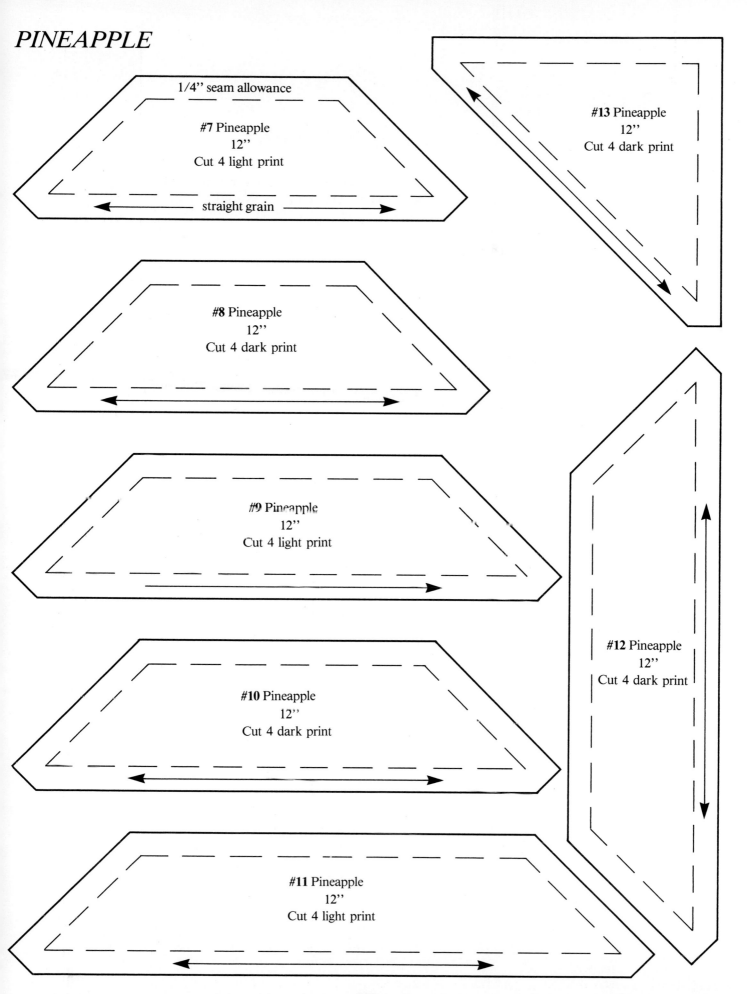

1/4" seam allowance

#7 Pineapple
12"
Cut 4 light print

straight grain

#8 Pineapple
12"
Cut 4 dark print

#9 Pineapple
12"
Cut 4 light print

#10 Pineapple
12"
Cut 4 dark print

#11 Pineapple
12"
Cut 4 light print

#13 Pineapple
12"
Cut 4 dark print

#12 Pineapple
12"
Cut 4 dark print

OVERALL PATTERNS

There are templates for six blocks that form overall patterns in this section of the book: Bow Tie, Double Wedding Ring, Grandmother's Flower Garden, Hexagon Stars, Spider Web, and Triangles. The blocks range in size from 4" to 14" and can be used in both wall hangings and full-size quilts.

These blocks are joined together without lattice to form a secondary design at the corners where the blocks meet and a repeating overall design. Most of the blocks are irregular in shape with the exception of Spider Web and Bow Tie which is shown in a lattice set on page 69.

Many of these blocks date back to the Victorian era, when quilts from these patterns were made from silks, satins and velvet scraps. These quilts used the English Paper Piecing Method of construction because the fabrics were both fragile and slippery. This method is still used today for blocks like Grandmother's Flower Garden, Hexagon Stars, and Spider Web.

Paper Piecing Method:

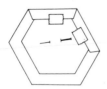 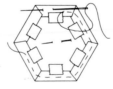 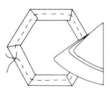

Lay patch right side down and pin a paper template to center. Fold fabric edge over and secure with tape.

Tack all around the patch and carefully remove the masking tape.

Press the fabric folds—this makes sewing the patches much easier.

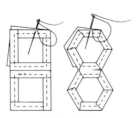 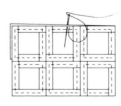 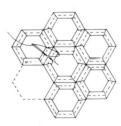

Individual patches are first joined with tiny overcasting stitches.

Next the patches are joined into rows, with overcasting stitches.

Hexagons can either be joined in rows or formed into rosettes.

BOW TIE

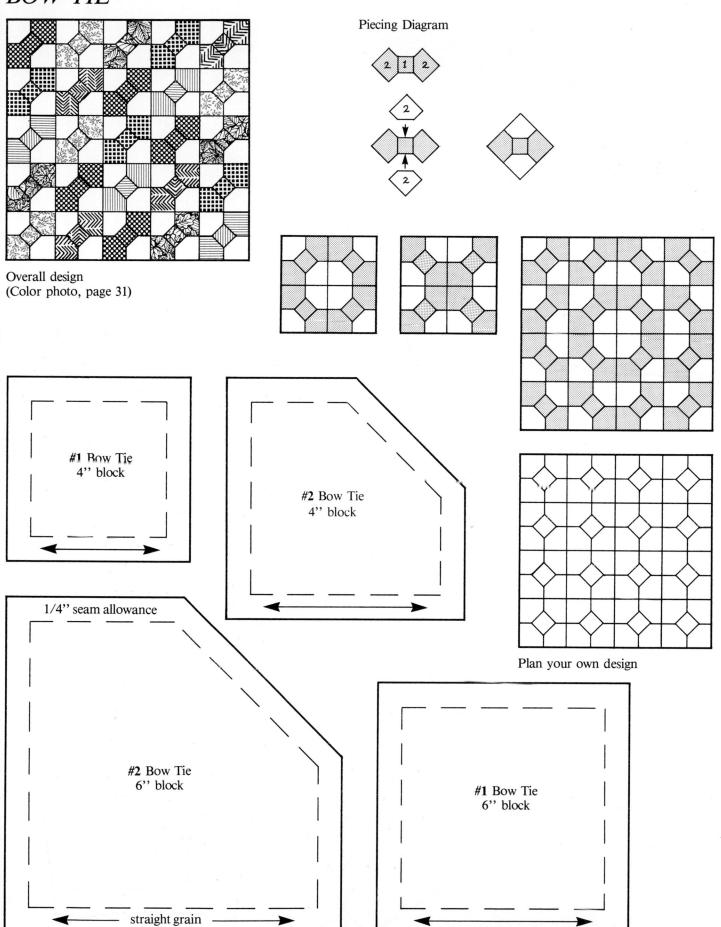

Overall design
(Color photo, page 31)

Piecing Diagram

#1 Bow Tie
4" block

#2 Bow Tie
4" block

1/4" seam allowance

#2 Bow Tie
6" block

straight grain

Plan your own design

#1 Bow Tie
6" block

DOUBLE WEDDING RING

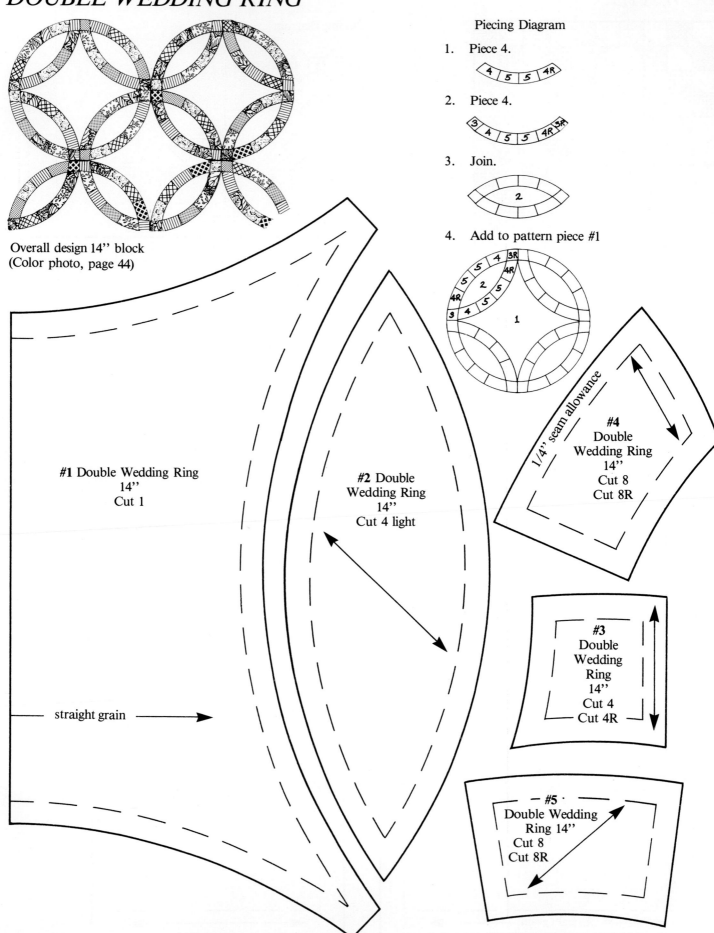

Overall design 14'' block
(Color photo, page 44)

Piecing Diagram

1. Piece 4.

   4 5 5 4R

2. Piece 4.

   3 4 5 5 4R 3R

3. Join.

   2

4. Add to pattern piece #1

#1 Double Wedding Ring
14''
Cut 1

straight grain →

#2 Double
Wedding Ring
14''
Cut 4 light

1/4'' seam allowance

#4
Double
Wedding Ring
14''
Cut 8
Cut 8R

#3
Double
Wedding
Ring
14''
Cut 4
Cut 4R

#5 ·
Double Wedding
Ring 14''
Cut 8
Cut 8R

GRANDMOTHER'S FLOWER GARDEN

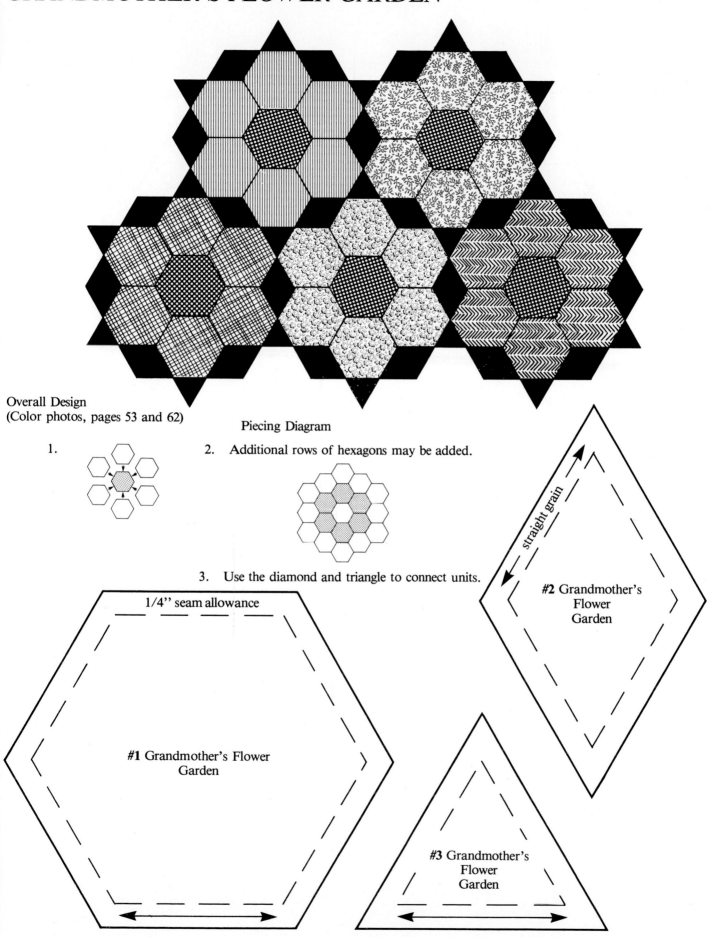

Overall Design
(Color photos, pages 53 and 62)

Piecing Diagram

1.

2.   Additional rows of hexagons may be added.

3.   Use the diamond and triangle to connect units.

straight grain

#2 Grandmother's
Flower
Garden

1/4'' seam allowance

#1 Grandmother's Flower
Garden

#3 Grandmother's
Flower
Garden

HEXAGON STARS

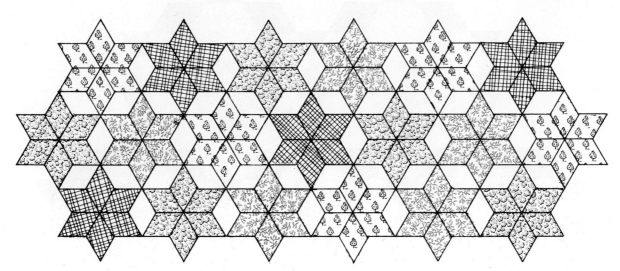

Overall Design
(Color photo, page 63)

Piecing Diagram

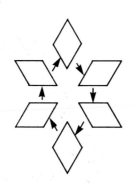

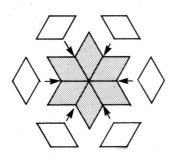

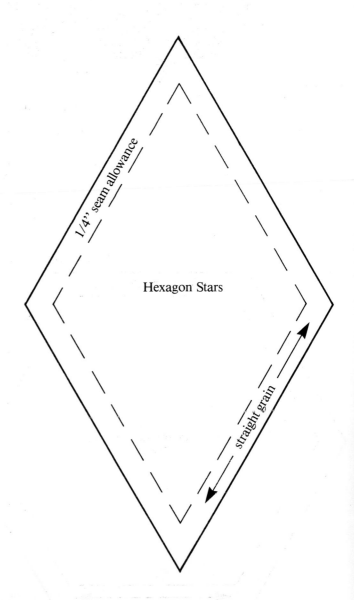

1/4" seam allowance

Hexagon Stars

straight grain

SPIDER WEB©

8" block
(Color photo, page 35)

Overall repeat.

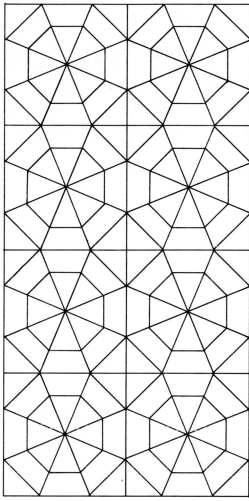

Piecing Diagram

Make 4   Make 4

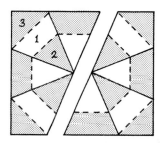

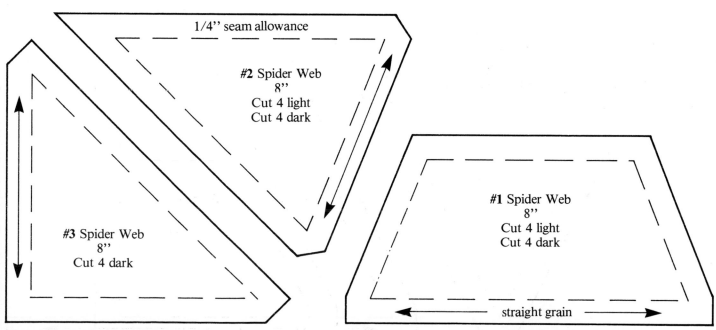

1/4" seam allowance

#2 Spider Web
8"
Cut 4 light
Cut 4 dark

#3 Spider Web
8"
Cut 4 dark

#1 Spider Web
8"
Cut 4 light
Cut 4 dark

straight grain

TRIANGLES

Overall repeat (Color photo, page 52)

Piecing Diagram

1.

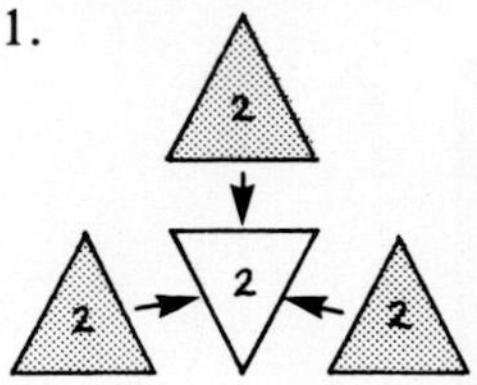

2. Alternate blocks.

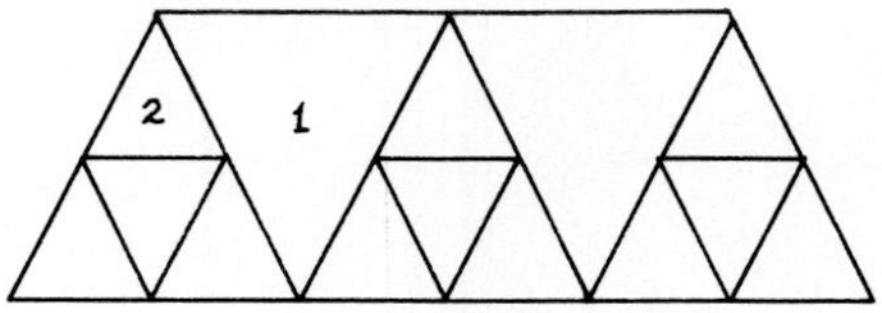

3. Use #3 to construct half blocks for edges.

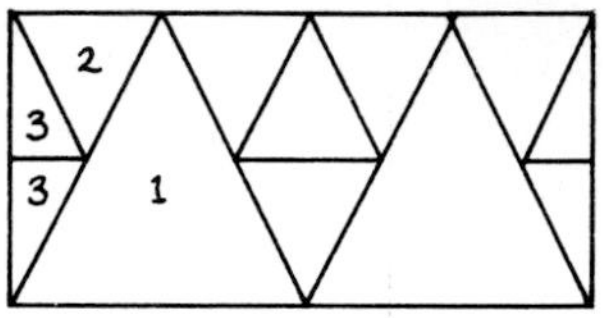

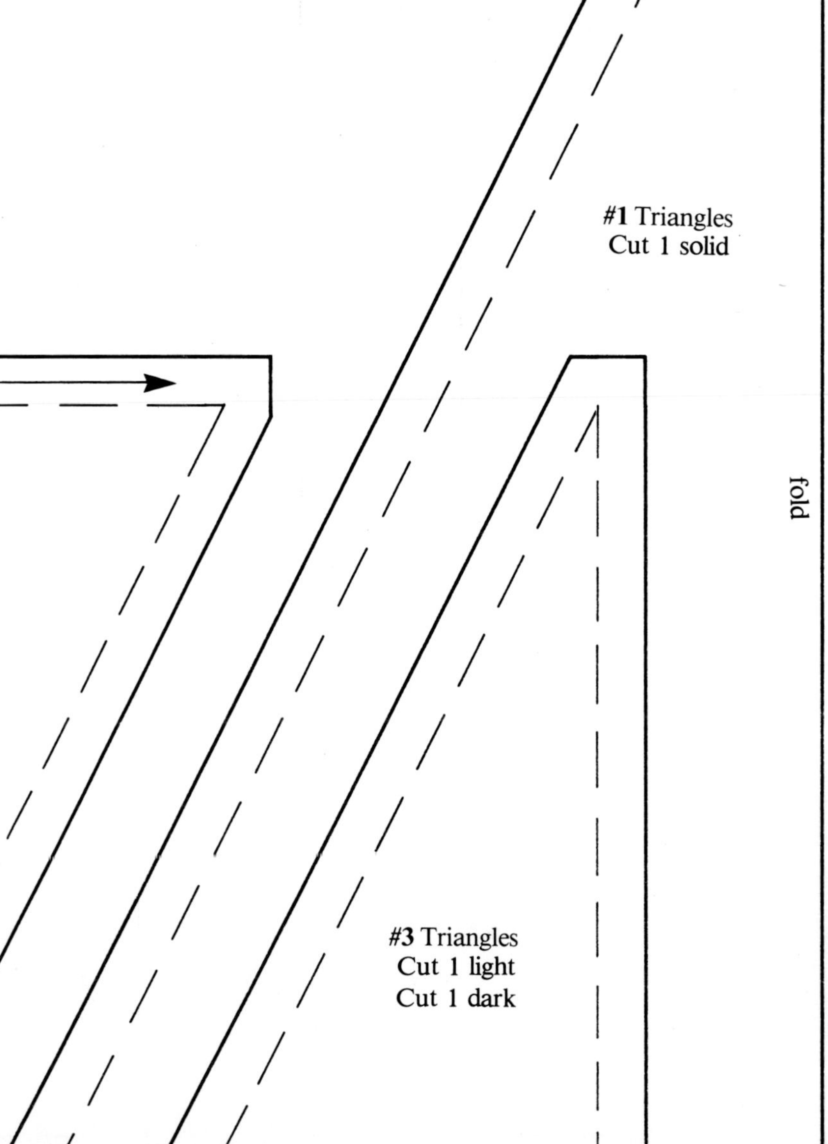

#1 Triangles
Cut 1 solid

#2 Triangles
Cut 1 light
Cut 3 dark

#3 Triangles
Cut 1 light
Cut 1 dark

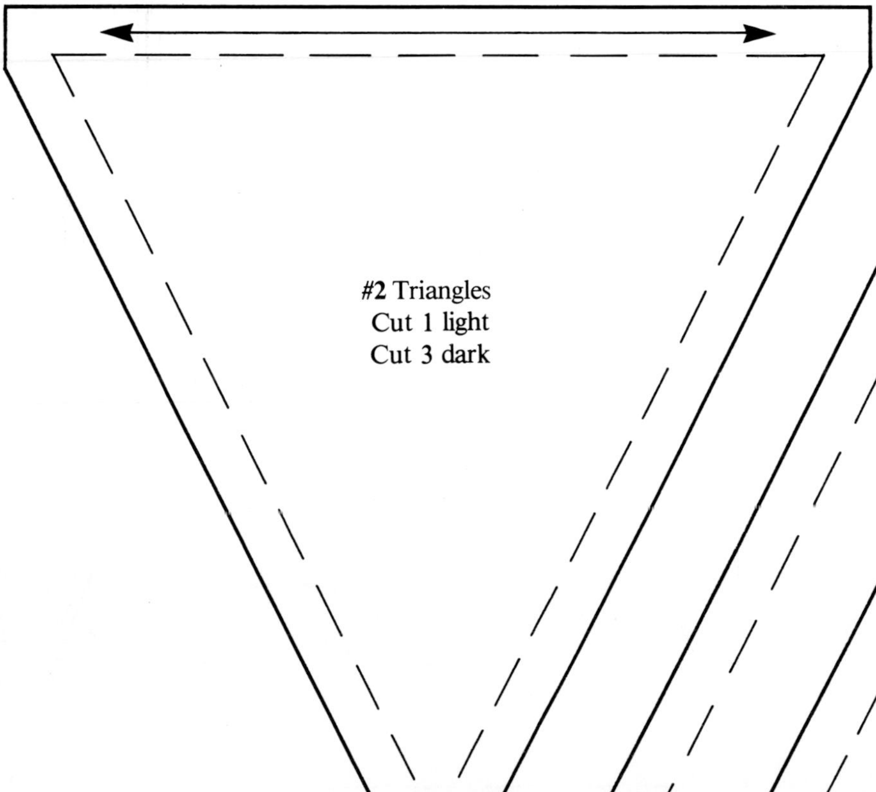

fold

APPLIQUE PATTERNS

There are pattern pieces given for eight applique blocks in this section of the book: Bed of Peonies, President's Wreath, Dresden Plate, Rose of Sharon, and Overall Bill and Sunbonnet Sue in two sizes. The blocks range in size from 6" to 14" and can be used in both wall hangings and full-size quilts.

Study the quilt plans found on pages 103-106 and adapt one to your block. Use the templates provided and the easy Paper Patch Applique technique to complete your block.

Paper Patch Applique

This easy technique will help beginners produce finished applique work.

1. Make templates for all pattern pieces from medium weight bond paper. Do not add seam allowance.
2. Place templates on fabric and draw 1/4" from all edges of template with an appropriate marking device.
3. Cut all fabric pieces along the drawn line.
4. Pin fabric to template.
5. Fold 1/4" seam allowances over template. Baste fabric to template, using a running stitch and sewing through the paper.
6. Clip inner curves and indentations, gently stretching fabric.
7. On outer curves, ease in fullness, using a small running stitch to gather the fabric. Do not sew through paper on outer curves. The basting stitches that go through the paper on either end of the outer curve will hold the fabric to the paper.
8. Baste all fabric pieces to paper. Do not use a knot after the last basting stitches since the basting stitches and paper must be removed in a later step.
9. Press all fabric pieces, easing fabric to ensure that bumpy edges are not created during pressing.
10. Applique fabric pieces to background, using a small blind stitch and matching thread. Applique tips can be found on page 150 of the Glossary of Techniques.

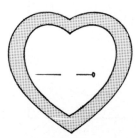

Pin paper to fabric.

Baste fabric to paper, sewing through paper.

Ease in fullness on curves with small running stitch.

Blind stitch fabric to background.

BED OF PEONIES

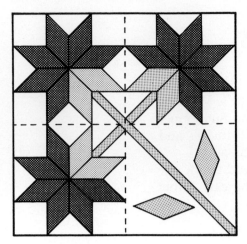

14" block (Color photo, page 67)

Piecing Sequence

1.   Make 6   Make 3   Make 3

A   B   C

Points indicated by arrows are set-in seams. Sew only up to 1/4" seam allowance and backtack.

2.   Flower units

     Make 3

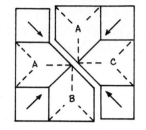

3.   Set the three flower units together with piece #4.

4.   Applique stem and leaves in place. (Applique stem is 3/4"-wide finished.)

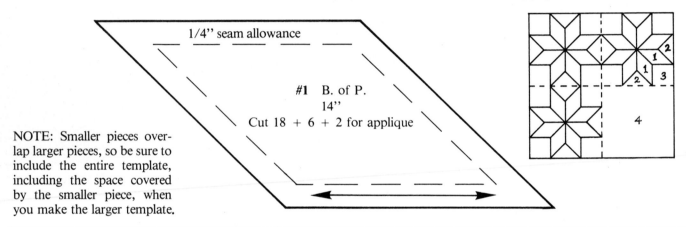

1/4" seam allowance

#1   B. of P.
14"
Cut 18 + 6 + 2 for applique

NOTE: Smaller pieces over-lap larger pieces, so be sure to include the entire template, including the space covered by the smaller piece, when you make the larger template.

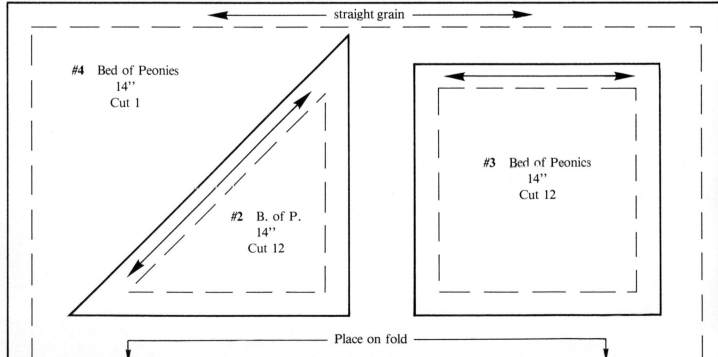

straight grain

#4   Bed of Peonies
14"
Cut 1

#2   B. of P.
14"
Cut 12

#3   Bed of Peonies
14"
Cut 12

Place on fold

DRESDEN PLATE

14" block
(Color photo, page 61)

1. Cut a 15" square of background fabric, (trim to size after applique is finished) fold both ways and crease the folds. Fold diagonally and crease.
2. Use the Paper Patch Applique technique shown on page 137 for the 16 segments.
3. Whipstitch together along the straight edge.
4. Applique to background fabric, aligning with creases.
5. Use Paper Patch Applique for Center.

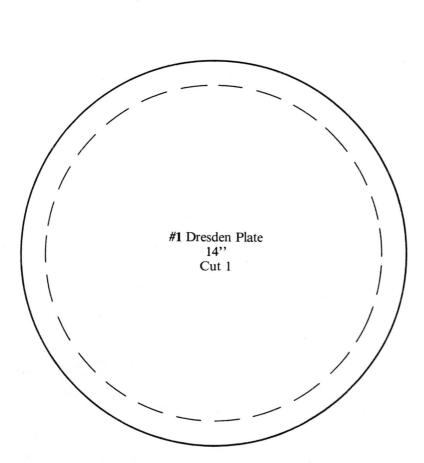

#1 Dresden Plate
14"
Cut 1

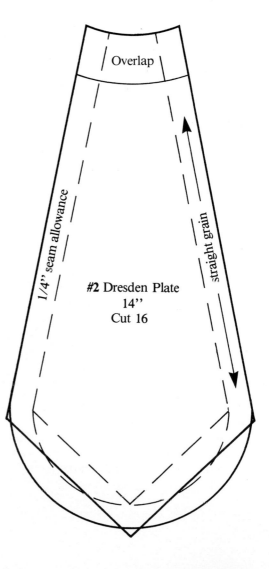

Overlap

1/4" seam allowance

straight grain

#2 Dresden Plate
14"
Cut 16

PRESIDENT'S WREATH

Cut a 15" square of background fabric, (trim to size after applique is finished), fold it in half both ways and press the folds. Fold diagonally and crease. Position the flowers on these creases. To help position the stems, use a compass set at 4.5" to draw a very light pencil circle on the fabric square. See page 137 for further instructions for Paper Patch Applique.

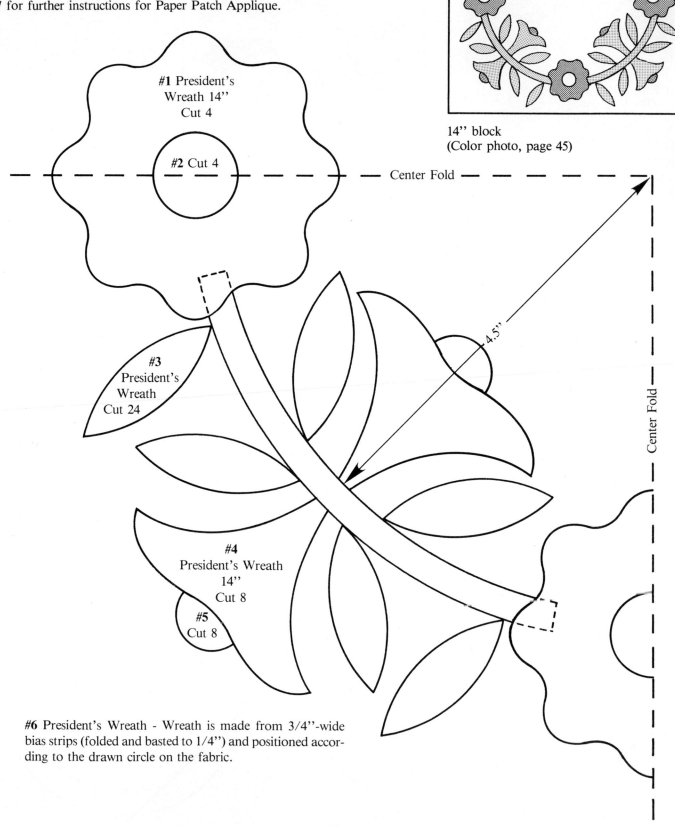

14" block
(Color photo, page 45)

#1 President's
Wreath 14"
Cut 4

#2 Cut 4

Center Fold

4.5"

Center Fold

#3
President's
Wreath
Cut 24

#4
President's Wreath
14"
Cut 8

#5
Cut 8

#6 President's Wreath - Wreath is made from 3/4"-wide bias strips (folded and basted to 1/4") and positioned according to the drawn circle on the fabric.

ROSE OF SHARON

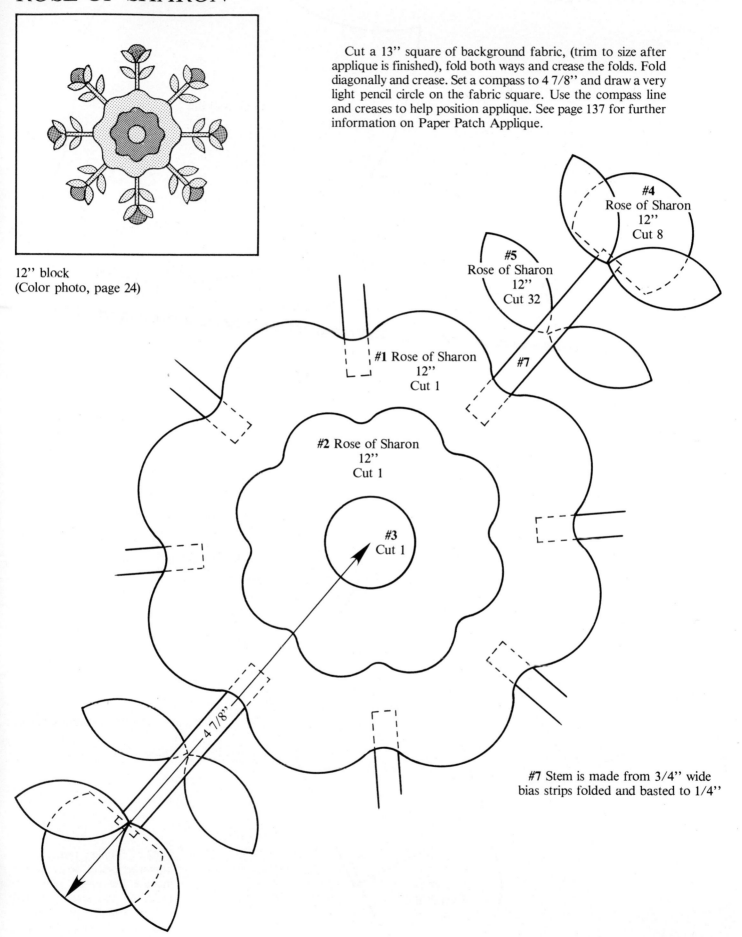

12" block
(Color photo, page 24)

Cut a 13" square of background fabric, (trim to size after applique is finished), fold both ways and crease the folds. Fold diagonally and crease. Set a compass to 4 7/8" and draw a very light pencil circle on the fabric square. Use the compass line and creases to help position applique. See page 137 for further information on Paper Patch Applique.

#4
Rose of Sharon
12"
Cut 8

#5
Rose of Sharon
12"
Cut 32

#1 Rose of Sharon
12"
Cut 1

#7

#2 Rose of Sharon
12"
Cut 1

#3
Cut 1

4 7/8"

#7 Stem is made from 3/4" wide
bias strips folded and basted to 1/4"

OVERALL BILL

12" block

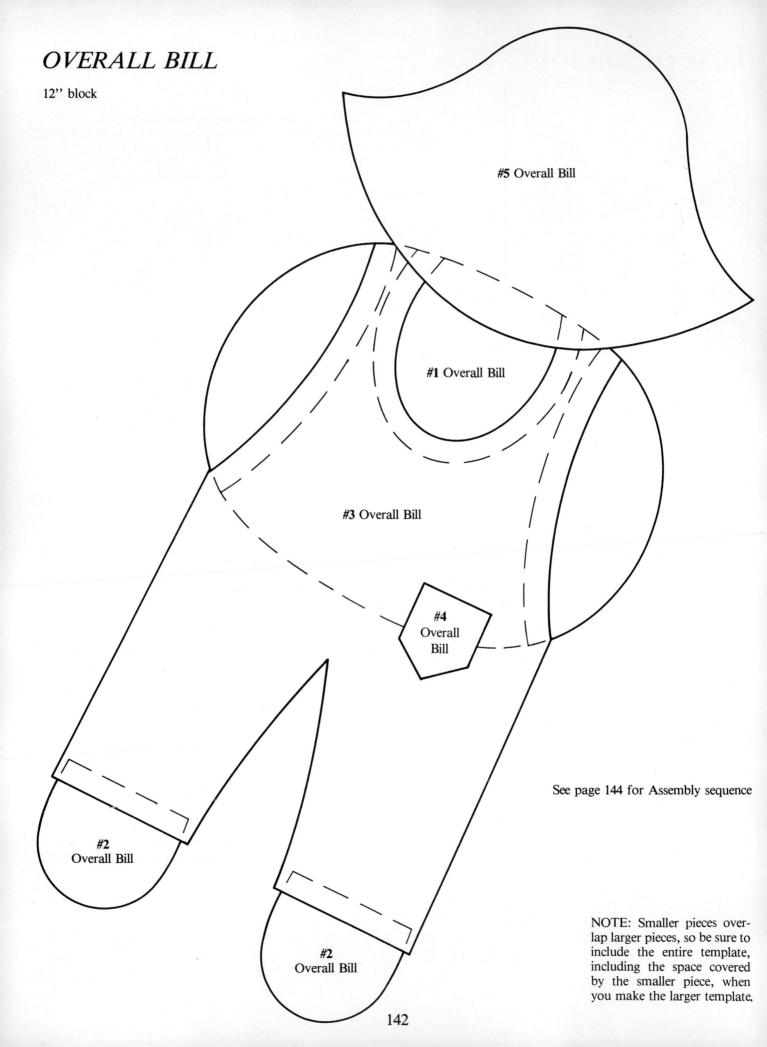

#5 Overall Bill

#1 Overall Bill

#3 Overall Bill

#4 Overall Bill

#2 Overall Bill

#2 Overall Bill

See page 144 for Assembly sequence

NOTE: Smaller pieces overlap larger pieces, so be sure to include the entire template, including the space covered by the smaller piece, when you make the larger template.

142

SUNBONNET SUE

12" block
(Color photo, page 59)

See page 144 for Assembly sequence.

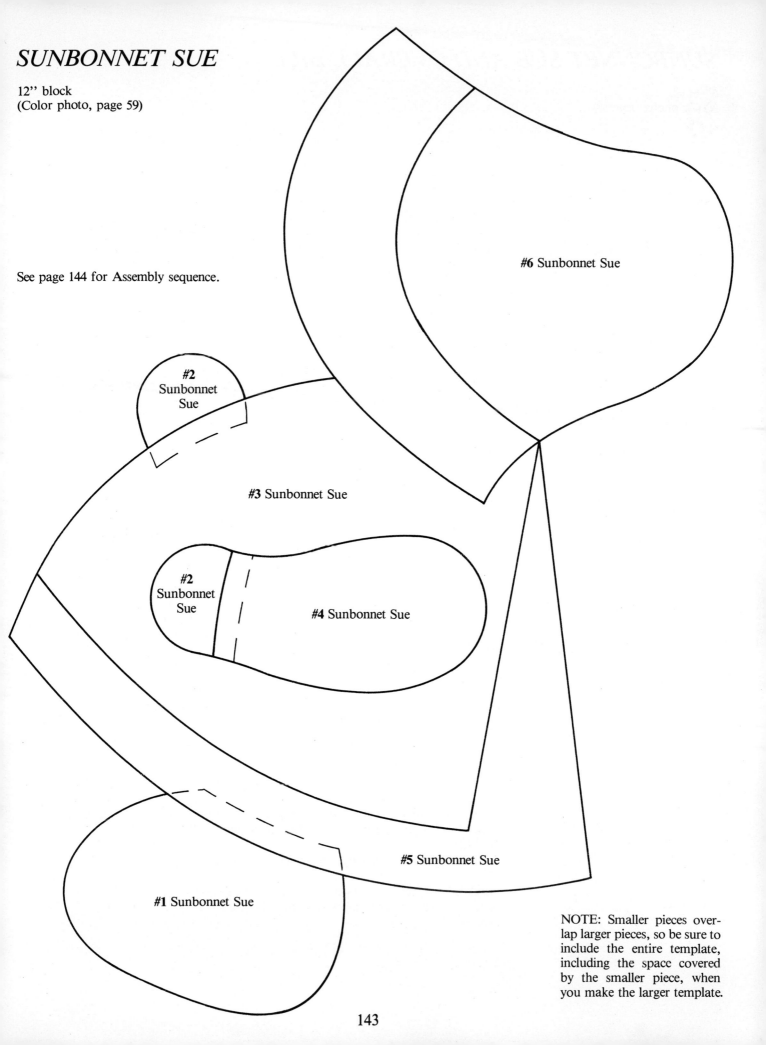

#2 Sunbonnet Sue

#6 Sunbonnet Sue

#3 Sunbonnet Sue

#2 Sunbonnet Sue

#4 Sunbonnet Sue

#5 Sunbonnet Sue

#1 Sunbonnet Sue

NOTE: Smaller pieces overlap larger pieces, so be sure to include the entire template, including the space covered by the smaller piece, when you make the larger template.

SUNBONNET SUE AND OVERALL BILL

6" block
(Color photo, page 59)

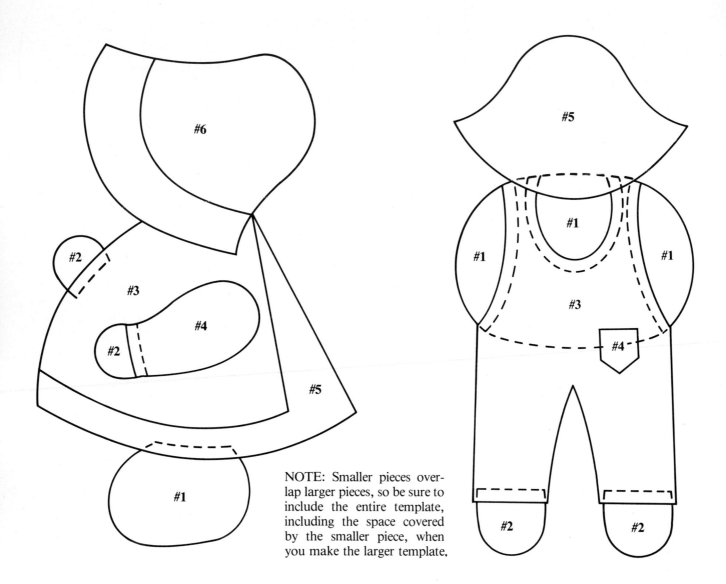

NOTE: Smaller pieces overlap larger pieces, so be sure to include the entire template, including the space covered by the smaller piece, when you make the larger template.

Assembly Sequence

1. Cut a 13" square of background fabric (7" square for small blocks). Block is trimmed to size after applique is finished.
2. Follow Paper Patch Applique directions given on page 137.
3. Begin with small pieces which are overlapped by larger pieces. Templates are numbered in the order they are appliqued.

GLOSSARY OF TECHNIQUES

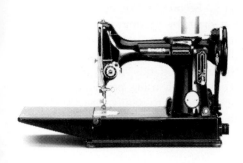

Tools and Supplies

Drawing Supplies: Graph paper in a 1/8" grid and colored pencils for drawing quilt plans and sketching design ideas.

Rulers: I use two rulers; both are clear plastic with a red grid of 1/8" squares. A short ruler is for drawing quilt designs on graph paper,; a longer one, 2" wide and 18" long, is for drafting designs full size, making templates, measuring and marking borders and quilting lines. If your local quilt shop doesn't carry them, try a stationery store or any place that carries drafting or art supplies. Another useful tool is a 12" plastic 45°/90° right angle.

Scissors: You will need scissors for paper, a good sharp pair for cutting fabric only, and possibly a little pair for snipping threads. If your fabric scissors are dull, have them sharpened. If they are close to "dead", invest in a new pair. It's worth it.

Template Material: To make templates, you will need graph paper or tracing paper, lightweight posterboard (manila file folders are good) or plastic, and a glue stick.

Markers: Most marking on fabric can be done with a regular #2 lead pencil and a white dressmaker's pencil. Keep them sharp. There is a blue felt tip marking pen available that is water erasable; it works especially well for marking quilting designs. (When you no longer need the lines for guides, spray them with cool water and the blue marks will disappear.) Ask the salespeople at a local fabric or quilt shop about the different kinds of marking pens available.

Sewing Machine: It needn't be fancy. All you need is an evenly locking straight stitch. Whatever kind of sewing machine you have, get to know it and how it runs. If it needs servicing, have it done, or get out the manual and do it yourself. Replace the old needle with a new one. Often, if your machine has a zigzag stitch, it will have a throat plate with an oblong hole for the needle to pass through. You might want to replace this plate with one that has a little round hole for straight stitching. This will help eliminate problems you might have with the edges of fabrics being fed into the hole by the action of the feed dogs.

Needles: A supply of new sewing machine needles for light to medium weight cottons is necessary. You'll also need an assortment of Sharps for handwork and quilting needles (Between #8, #9 or #10) if you plan to hand quilt.

Pins: Multi-colored glass or plastic-headed pins are generally longer, stronger and easier to see and hold than regular dressmaker's pins.

Iron and Ironing Board: A shot of steam is useful.

Seam Ripper: I always keep one handy.

Cutting

Study the design and templates. Determine the number of pieces to cut of each shape and each fabric. Trim the selvage from the fabric before you begin cutting. When one fabric is to be used both for borders and in the unit block designs, cut the borders first and the smaller pieces from what is left over (see Borders on page 43).

At the ironing board, press and fold the fabric so that one, two or four layers can be cut at one time (except for linear prints such as stripes and checks that should be cut one at a time). Fold the fabric so that each piece will be cut on the straight grain.

Position stiffened templates on the fabric so the arrows match the straight grain of the fabric. With a sharp pencil (white for dark fabrics, lead for light ones), trace around the template on the fabric. This is the cutting line. Cut just inside this line to most accurately duplicate the template.

In machine piecing, there are no drawn lines to guide your sewing. The seamline is 1/4" from the cut edge of the fabric, so this outside edge must be precisely cut to ensure accurate sewing.

Machine Piecing

For machine piecing, use white or neutral thread as light in color as the lightest fabric in the project. Use a dark neutral thread for piecing dark solids. It is easier to work with 100% cotton thread on some machines. Check your needle. If it is dull, burred or bent, replace it with a fresh one.

Sew exact 1/4" seams. To determine the 1/4" seam allowance on your machine, place a template under the presser foot and gently lower the needle onto the seamline. The distance from the needle to the edge of the template is 1/4". Lay a piece of masking tape at the edge of the template to act as the 1/4" mark; use the edge as a guide. Stitch length should be set at 10-12 stitches per inch. For most of the sewing in this book, sew from cut edge to cut edge (exceptions will be noted). Backtack, if you wish, although it is really not necessary as each seam will be crossed and held by another.

Use chain piecing whenever possible to save time and thread. To chain piece, sew one seam, but do not lift the presser foot. Do not take the piece out of the sewing machine and do not cut the thread. Instead, set up the next seam to be sewn and stitch as you did the first. There will be a little twist of thread between the two pieces. Sew all the seams you can at one time in this way, then remove the "chain". Clip the threads.

Press the seam allowances to one side, toward the darker fabric when possible. Avoid too much ironing as you sew because it tends to stretch biases and distort fabric shapes.

To piece a block, sew the smallest pieces together first to form units. Join smaller units to form larger ones until the block is complete.

Chain piecing

Short seams need not be pinned unless matching is involved, or the seam is longer than 4''. Keep pins away from the seamline. Sewing over pins tends to burr the needle and makes it hard to be accurate in tight places.

Here are six matching techniques that can be helpful in many different piecing situations.

1. Opposing Seams: When stitching one seamed unit to another, press seam allowances on the seams that need to match in opposite directions. The two "opposing" seams will hold each other in place and evenly distribute the bulk. Plan pressing to take advantage of opposing seams.

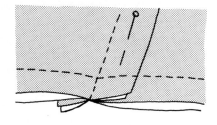

2. Positioning Pin: A pin, carefully pushed straight through two points that need to match and pulled tight, will establish the proper point of matching. Pin the seam normally and remove the positioning pin before stitching.

Positioning pin

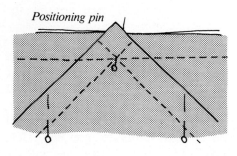

3. The "X" : When triangles are pieced, stitches will form an "X" at the next seamline. Stitch through the center of the "X" to make sure the points on the sewn triangles will not be chopped off.

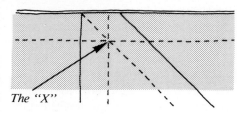

The "X"

4. Easing: When two pieces to be sewn together are supposed to match but instead are slightly different lengths, pin the points of matching and stitch with the shorter piece on top. The feed dogs ease the fullness of the bottom piece.

Set-in seams

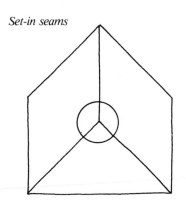

5. Set-in seams: Where three seam lines come together at an angle, stop all stitching at the 1/4'' seam line and backtack. Don't let even one stitch extend into the seam allowance. As each seam is finished, take the work out of the machine, position the next seam and start stitching in the new direction. Backtacking is necessary because these seamlines will not be crossed and held by any other stitches.

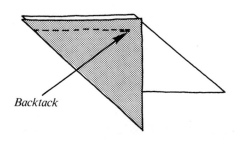

Backtack

6. Making Eight Points Come Together: To make eight points come together crisply as needed in the Whirlygig block and many others, follow these three steps: First, chain piece light and dark triangles together to form four squares. Press each seam towards the dark. Second, make two halves of the pinwheel by sewing two square units together as shown. Match using opposing diagonal seams. Press each new seam towards the dark. Third, sew the center seam. Match using positioning pin and opposing seams. Stitch exactly through the "X".

Strip Piecing

Strip piecing is a method for sewing patchwork units together quickly by machine. Long fabric strips are sewn together in units called strata and then cut into shorter portions; the small units are then recombined to form simple designs.

Four Patch Units

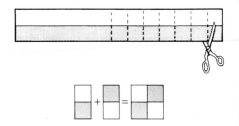

Ninepatch Units

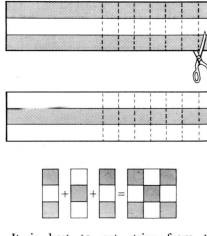

It is best to cut strips from the lengthwise grain of the fabric. When it is necessary to use the cross-grain to get the required length, be sure to straighten the fabric so strips will be cut exactly on-grain.

Press the fabric well before cutting strips. The accuracy of the piecing will depend largely on how carefully fabric, strips and seams are pressed.

To determine the width to cut strips, add a 1/4" seam allowance to each side of the finished strip. For example, if the finished dimension of the piece will be 1", cut 1 1/2" strips. Stack the fabric before marking and cutting so two or four layers can be cut at one time. Mark strips and cut with sharp scissors or a rotary cutter. Try to be accurate; speed piecing does not mean sloppy piecing.

Sew long strips together with 1/4" seam allowances, but wait to press until all the strips in the unit have been sewn. Press seam allowances toward the darker fabric, and press from the right side of the work so the fabric won't pleat along the seamlines. Use templates or simply measure distances to mark locations for crosswise cuts.

Bias-Strip Piecing

Use bias-strip piecing when working with triangles. Half-square triangles and quarter-square triangles, as well as many other shapes, can be cut using this method. It is extremely accurate and especially useful for very small half-square units like the "feathers" on a Feathered Star.

Half-square triangles

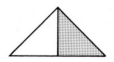

Quarter-square triangles

Making bias strips

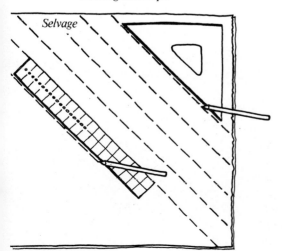

Begin by cutting two strips of bias grain fabric, one dark and one light.

Layer the two fabrics, mark the top layer as shown, and cut two strips at a time. To determine the width of the bias strips, measure the square template to be used from corner to corner (including seam allowances) on the diagonal. Add 3" and divide by 2.

$$\frac{X" + 3"}{2} = \text{width of each bias strip}$$

Sew the strips together on the long bias edge, using 1/4" seam allowance. Press seams open or toward the dark fabric. Place a stiffened square template on the right side of the bias strip unit with opposite corners lined up with the seamline. Trace around the template. Start at one end and make a string of squares the length of the seamline. Carefully cut out the fabric squares, cutting only on the drawn lines (actually right inside the drawn lines). This will yield several squares made of two triangles with outside edges on the straight grain of the fabric. There will be two funny shaped pieces left over. Seam the long straight edges of these together, press, and make another set of squares.

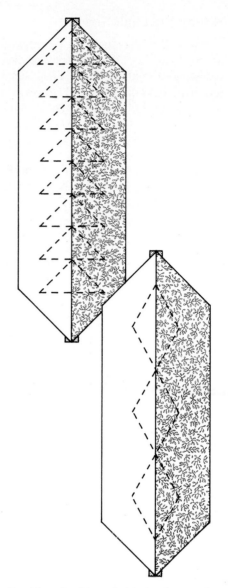

Consider using bias-strip piecing for any shape consisting of two equal triangles.

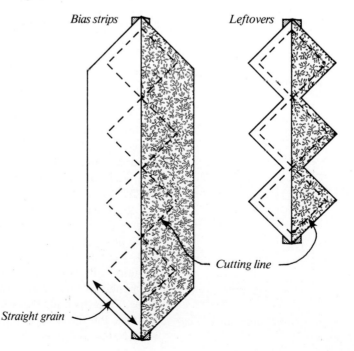

147

Setting the Quilt Together

When all of the blocks are pieced, you are ready to "set" the quilt top together, following a setting plan. First stitch together blocks or blocks and lattices into rows, using ¼" seams. Then stitch together rows of blocks or rows of blocks and lattice strips. Setting sequences are shown in diagrams.

When the center portion is pieced together, borders may then be added to the quilt.

Lattice squares are pieced to lattice. Lattice strips are pieced around quilt blocks. Join rows of lattice strips and squares to rows of quilt blocks and lattice.

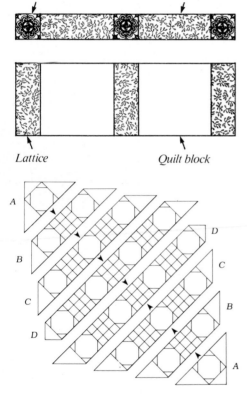

Assembly sequence of diagonally set quilt.

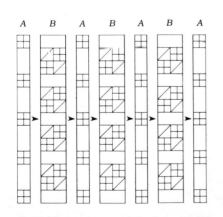

Assembly sequence with lattices and "Four Patch" set pieces.

Mitering Corners

1. Prepare the borders. Determine the finished outside dimensions of your quilt. Cut the borders this length plus 1/2" for seam allowances. When using a striped fabric for the borders, make sure the design on all four borders is cut the same way. Multiple borders should be sewn together and the resulting "striped" units treated as a single border for mitering.

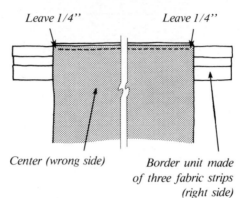

Center (wrong side)

Border unit made of three fabric strips (right side)

2. To attach the border to the pieced section of the quilt, center each border on a side so the ends extend equally on either side of the center section. Using a 1/4" seam allowance, sew the border to the center leaving 1/4" unsewn at the beginning and end of the stitching line. Press the seam allowances toward the border.

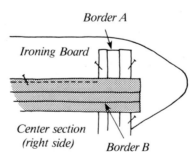

3. Arrange the first corner to be mitered on the ironing board as illustrated. Press the corner flat and straight. To prevent it from slipping, pin the quilt to the ironing board. Following the illustration, turn border "B" right side up, folding the corner to be mitered under at a 45° angle. Match the raw edges underneath with those of border "A". Fuss with it until it looks good. The stripes and border designs should meet. Check the squareness of the corner with a right angle. Press the fold. This will be the sewing line. Pin the borders together to prevent shifting and unpin the piece from the

board. Turn wrong side out and pin along the fold line, readjusting if necessary to match the designs.

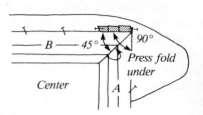

4. Machine baste from the inside to the outside corner on the fold line, leaving 1/4" at the beginning unsewn. Check for accuracy. If it is right, sew again with a regular stitch. Backtack at the beginning and end of the stitching line. (After you have mitered several times, the basting step ceases to be necessary.) Trim the excess fabric 1/4" along the mitered seam. Press this seam open. Press the other seams to the outside.

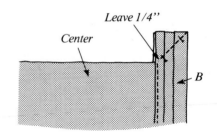

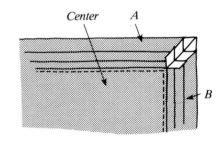

Preparing to Quilt

Marking

In most cases, before you quilt, the quilt top must be marked with lines to guide stitching. Where you place the quilting lines will depend on the patchwork design, the type of batting used, and how much quilting you want to do.

Try to avoid quilting too close to the seamlines, where the bulk of seam allowances might slow you down or make the stitches uneven. Keep in mind also that the purpose of quilting, besides its esthetic value, is to securely hold the three layers together. Don't leave large areas unquilted.

Thoroughly press the quilt top and mark it before it is assembled with the batting and backing. You will need marking pencils, a long ruler or yardstick, stencils or templates for quilting motifs, and a smooth, clean hard surface on which to work. Use a sharp marking pencil and lightly mark the quilting lines on the fabric. No matter what kind of marking tool is used, light lines will be easier to remove than heavy ones.

Backing

A single length of 45"-wide fabric can often be used for backing small quilts. To be safe, plan on a useable width of only 42" after shrinkage and cutting off selvages. For larger quilts, two lengths of fabric will have to be sewn together to get a large enough backing.

Cut the backing an inch larger than the quilt top all the way around. Press thoroughly with seams open. Lay the backing face down on a large, clean, flat surface. With masking tape, tape the backing down (without stretching) to keep it smooth and flat while you are working with the other layers.

Batting

Batting is the filler in a quilt or comforter. Thick batting is used in comforters that are tied. If you plan to quilt, use thin batting and quilt by hand.

Thin batting comes in 100% polyester, 100% cotton and a cotton-polyester (80%-20%) combination. All cotton batting requires close quilting to prevent shifting and separating in the wash. Most old quilts have cotton batting and are rather flat. Cotton is a good natural fiber that lasts well and is compatible with cotton and cotton-blend fabrics. Less quilting is required on 100% polyester batting. If polyester batting is glazed or bonded, it is easy to work with, won't pull apart and has more loft than cotton. Some polyester batting, however, has a tendency to "beard". This "fiber migration" (the small white polyester fibers creep to the quilt's surface between the threads in the fabric) happens mostly when polyester blends are used instead of 100% cotton fabrics. The cotton-polyester combination batting is supposed to combine the best features of the two fibers. A single layer of preshrunk cotton flannel can be used for filler instead of batting. The quilt will be very flat, and the quilting stitches highly visible.

Cut the batting the same size as the quilt backing and lay it gently on top.

Assembling the Layers

Center the freshly ironed and marked quilt top on top of the batting, face up. Starting in the middle, pin baste the three layers together while gently smoothing out fullness to the sides and corners. Take care not to distort the straight lines of the quilt design and the borders.

After pinning, baste the layers together with needle and light colored thread. Start in the middle and make a line of large stitches to each corner to form a large X. Continue basting in a grid of parallel lines 6" to 8" apart. Finish with a row of basting around the outside edges. Quilts to be quilted with a hoop or on your lap will be handled more than those quilted on a frame; therefore, they will require more basting.

After basting, remove the pins. Now you are ready to quilt.

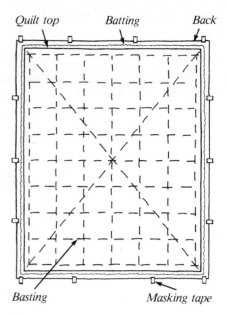

Quilt top   *Batting*   *Back*

Basting   *Masking tape*

Hand Quilting

To quilt by hand, you will need quilting thread, quilting needles, small scissors, a thimble and perhaps a balloon or large rubber band to help grasp the needle if it gets stuck. Quilt on a frame, a large hoop, or just on your lap or a table. Use a single strand of quilting thread no longer than 18". Make a small single knot in the end of the thread. The quilting stitch is a small running stitch that goes through all three layers of the quilt. Take two, three or even four stitches at a time if you can keep them even. When crossing seams, you might find it necessary to "hunt and peck" one stitch at a time.

To begin, insert the needle in the top layer about 3/4" from the point you want to start stitching. Pull the needle out at the starting point and gently tug at the knot until it pops through the fabric and is buried in the batting. Make a backstitch and begin quilting. Stitches should be tiny (8 to 10 per inch is good), even and straight. At first, concentrate on even and straight; tiny will come with practice.

When you come almost to the end of the thread, make a single knot fairly close to the fabric. Make a backstitch to bury the knot in the batting. Run the thread off through the batting and out the quilt top. Snip it off. The first and last stitches look different from the running stitches between. To make them less noticeable, start and stop where quilting lines cross each other or at seam joints.

Hand quilting stitch

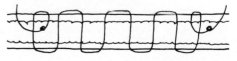

Binding

After quilting, trim excess batting and backing to the edge of the quilt front. Finish the raw edges with bias binding. Bias binding can be purchased by the package or by the yard, or you can make your own.

To make bias binding from yardage, press a single layer of fabric. Use a 12" right angle to establish the bias (45° angle) of the fabric by aligning one of the angle's short sides with the selvage. Draw a line on the fabric along the 45° angle. Using this first marked line as a guide, draw several more parallel lines, each 2" apart. You'll find the 2"-wide plastic ruler very handy for this procedure. Cut the strips and seam them together where necessary to get a bias strip long enough for each side of the quilt (the length of the side plus 2").

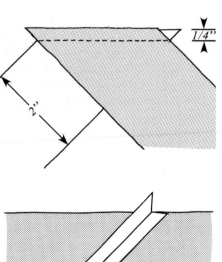

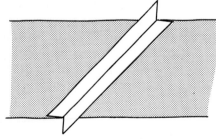

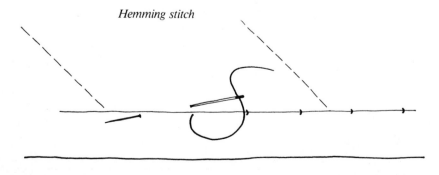

Hemming stitch

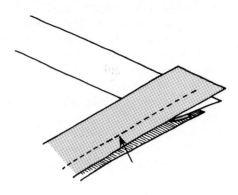

Overlapping bias binding at quilt corners

Using the "even-feed" presser foot and a 1/2" seam allowance, sew the binding strips to the front of the quilt. Be careful not to stretch the bias or the quilt edge as you sew. If your machine doesn't have an "even-feed" foot, sometimes it is best to put the binding on entirely by hand. Overlap the corners. Fold under the raw edge of the binding on the back side of the quilt. Pin it in place. Enclose the raw edges at the corners. Using thread to match the binding, hand sew the binding in place with a hemming stitch.

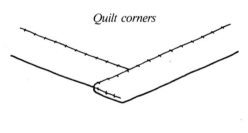

Quilt corners

Applique Tips

A. Avoid unsightly knots and thread ends by taking four or five running stitches through the foundation material under the edge of the applique piece. Then anchor the thread end at the edge so there is no chance of it being cut when you cut the foundation fabric.

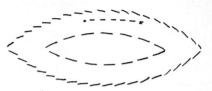

B. After anchoring the thread, bring the needle straight up from the back through the foundation fabric, catching a few threads of the applique piece. Push the needle down through the foundation fabric only, very close to the point where the needle came up. If you move too far away from this point, your applique will look like a hem.

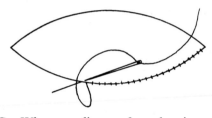

C. When applique of each piece is almost complete, pull basting thread from fabric and remove paper from the small opening that remains. A pair of tweezers is helpful for this step. If you completed the applique and forgot to remove the paper, make a small slit through the back side of the background fabric and remove paper with tweezers.

D. Cutting away the foundation fabric will make a big difference in the finished block. Separate the applique from the foundation fabric, then snip the foundation fabric just enough to slide the scissors inside. Trim 1/4" from the edge using the stitches as a guide. This will make the applique lie flatter, and eliminate the possibility of having to quilt through extra layers of material.

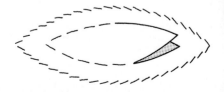

Bacon, Lenice. *American Patchwork Quilts.* New York: Bonanza Books, 1980.

Benberry, Cuesta. "The 20th Century's First Quilt Revival." *Quilter's Newsletter Magazine,* July/August 1979, pp. 20–21.

Benberry, Cuesta. "The 20th Century's First Quilt Revival." *Quilter's Newsletter Magazine,* September 1979, pp. 25–6, 29.

Benberry, Cuesta. "The 20th Century's First Quilt Revival." *Quilter's Newsletter Magazine,* October 1979, p. 10.

Beyer, Jinny. *The Quilter's Album of Blocks and Borders.* McLean, Va.: EPM Publications, Inc., 1980.

Brackman, Barbara. "Dating Old Quilts, Part Two: Cotton Prints up to 1890." *Quilter's Newsletter Magazine,* October 1984, p. 26.

Brackman, Barbara. "Dating Old Quilts, Part Three: Cotton Prints 1890–1960." *Quilter's Newsletter Magazine,* November 1984, p. 16.

Brackman, Barbara. "Patterns to Ponder." *Quiltworld Omnibook,* Winter 1983, p. 13.

Brackman, Barbara. "Patterns to Ponder." *Quiltworld Omnibook,* Summer 1985, p. 6.

Brackman, Barbara. "Patterns to Ponder." *Quiltworld Omnibook,* Fall, 1985, p. 6.

Brackman, Barbara. "Patterns to Ponder." *Quiltworld Omnibook,* Winter 1985, p. 6.

Bunyan, John. *Pilgrim's Progress.* New York: Macmillan Co., 1913.

Carroll, Amy, ed. *Patchwork and Applique.* New York: Ballantine Books, 1981.

Dubois, Jean. *The Colonial History Quilt.* Wheatridge, Co.: Leman Publications, 1976.

Faudry, Marguerite and Deborah Brown, *The Book of Samplers.* New York: St. Martin's Press, 1980.

Finley, Ruth E. *Old Patchwork Quilts and the Women Who Made Them.* Newton Center, Mass.: Charles T. Branford Company, 1983.

Fox, Sandi. *Small Endearments.* New York: Charles Scribner's Sons, 1985.

Gross, Joyce. "Cuesta Benberry: Part II Significant Milestones for Quilters." *Quilter's Journal,* No. 24, March 1984, pp. 24–6..

Hagerman, Betty J. *A Meeting of the Sunbonnet Children.* Baldwin City, Kans.: Betty J. Hagerman, 1979.

Hall, Carrie A. and Krestinger, Rose G. *The Romance of the Patchwork Quilt.* New York: Bonanza Books, 1935.

Holstein, Jonathan. *The Pieced Quilt: An American Design Tradition.* Greenwich, Conn.: New York Graphic Society, Ltd., 1973.

Horton, Roberta. *Calico and Beyond: The Use of Patterned Fabric in Quilts.* Lafayette, Calif.: C & T Publishing, 1986.

Irwin, John Rice. *A People and Their Quilts.* Exton, Pa.: Schiffer Publishing Company, 1983.

Jones, Karen M. *From A to Z: A Folk Art Alphabet.* New York: Mayflower Books, Inc., 1978.

Kowaleski, Marilyn. "Collectible Calicoes." *Country Living Magazine,* March 1985, p. 61.

Lasansky, Jeannette. *In the Heart of Pennsylvania.* Lewisburg, Pa.: Oral Traditions Project, 1985.

Leman, Bonnie and Judy Martin. *Log Cabin Quilts.* Wheatridge, Co.: Moon Over the Mountain Publishing Company, 1980.

Mainardi, Patricia. *Quilts: The Great American Art.* San Pedro, Calif.: Miles & Weir, 1978.

Marshall, Catherine. *Christy.* New York: McGraw-Hill, 1967.

Martin, Nancy. *Housing Projects.* Bothell, Wa.: That Patchwork Place, Inc., 1984.

McCloskey, Marsha R. *Small Quilts.* Bothell, Wa.: That Patchwork Place, Inc., 1982.

McCloskey, Marsha R. *Wall Quilts.* Bothell, Wa.: That Patchwork Place, Inc., 1983.

McCloskey, Marsha R. *Projects for Blocks and Borders.* Bothell, Wa.: That Patchwork Place, Inc., 1984.

McCloskey, Marsha R. *Christmas Quilts.* Bothell, Wa.: That Patchwork Place, Inc., 1985.

McKim, Ruby. *101 Patchwork Patterns.* New York: Dover Publications, Inc., 1962.

Nelson, Cyril I. and Houck, Carter. *The Quilt Engagement Calendar Treasury.* New York: E.P. Dutton, Inc., 1982.

Nelson, Cyril I. *The Quilt Engagement Calendar.* New York: E.P. Dutton, Inc., 1985.

Orlofsky, Patsy and Myron. *Quilts in America.* New York: McGraw-Hill, 1974.

Peto, Florence. *Historic Quilts.* New York: The American Historical Company, Inc., 1939.

Rumford, Beatrix T. *The Abby Aldrich Rockefeller Folk Art Collection.* Williamsburg, Va.: The Williamsburg Foundation, 1975.

Safford, Carleton L. and Bishop, Robert. *America's Quilts and Coverlets.* New York: Weathervane Books, 1974.

Sears Roebuck and Company Catalog, Fall 1900, pp. 590–91.

Sienkiewicz, Elly. *Spoken Without a Word.* Washington, D.C.: Turtle Hill Press, 1983.

Smith, Linda Joan. "A Legacy of Quilts." *Country Home Magazine,* February 1986, pp. 67, 69, 71.

Strasser, Susan. *Never Done: A History of American Housework.* New York: Pantheon Books, 1982.

Stratton, Joanna L. *Pioneer Women: Voices from the Kansas Frontier.* New York: Simon & Schuster, 1981.

Walker, Michele. *Quilting and Patchwork.* New York: Ballantine Books, 1983.

Webster, Marie D. *Quilts: Their Story and How to Make Them.* Garden City, N.Y.: Doubleday Page & Co., 1915.

Weiland, Barbara, ed. *Needlework Nostalgia.* New York: Butterwick Publishing, 1975.

INDEX

That Patchwork Place Publications

Nancy Martin, designer and author, began stitching at an early age. Nancy did embroidery as a child and began constructing clothing in her teen-age years. When her interest in patchwork and quilting developed, Nancy's first projects were quilted garments.

Utilizing her background in education, Nancy set about teaching the construction of patchwork and quilted garments through the publication of her "strip-quilted clothing patterns."

As president of That Patchwork Place, Inc., Nancy Martin holds publishing rights to 132 patterns and 38 instructional booklets which are marketed throughout the United States, Canada, Great Britain and Australia.

Nancy is aided by her husband, Dan, and a supportive staff of employees at That Patchwork Place, all quilt-oriented. She is active in her local historical society and two area quilt guilds, Quilters Anonymous and Block Party Quilters. Nancy is also a member of the American/International Quilt Association and is a past advisory board member of Quilt Market.